Philanthropic Foundations in International Development

This book focuses on the influence of philanthropic foundations in global development, and on how the global south has engaged with them.

The idea of corporate philanthropy stretches back a long way, with the late 19th industrialist Andrew Carnegie seeing it as an important obligation of the very wealthy. In the modern day, Bill Gates has taken up this call, suggesting that the very wealthy should donate half their wealth to philanthropic causes, and endowing his own foundation with something in the order of $50 billion. This book brings together case studies of the most influential of these foundations over the last 100 years: the Rockefeller, Ford, and Gates' Foundations, investigating their impact on education and research, health and agriculture. The book concludes by asking whether global south foundations such as Al Waleed Philanthropies, Tata Trusts, and those from China may point to the future of global philanthropic foundations.

The sheer scale of resources that foundations can devote to their work results in significant influence in global politics, to the point that Foundations can drive and even set government policy. This influence is likely to grow in the post-Covid environment, making this book an important resource for researchers, practitioners and policy makers working on global development.

Patrick Kilby is a Senior Lecturer at Australian National University and Adjunct Associate Professor, Humanitarian and Development Research Initiative (HADRI) at Western Sydney University.

Routledge Explorations in Development Studies

This Development Studies series features innovative and original research at the regional and global scale. It promotes interdisciplinary scholarly works drawing on a wide spectrum of subject areas, in particular politics, health, economics, rural and urban studies, sociology, environment, anthropology, and conflict studies.

Topics of particular interest are globalization; emerging powers; children and youth; cities; education; media and communication; technology development; and climate change.In terms of theory and method, rather than basing itself on any orthodoxy, the series draws broadly on the tool kit of the social sciences in general, emphasizing comparison, the analysis of the structure and processes, and the application of qualitative and quantitative methods.

Barriers to Effective Civil Society Organisations
Political, Social and Financial Shifts
Edited by Ibrahim Natil, Vanessa Malila and Youcef Sai

Media Power and Hegemony in South Africa
The Myth of Independence
Blessed Ngwenya

Economic Neoliberalism and International Development
Edited by Michael Tribe

Critical Reflections on Public Private Partnerships
Edited by Jasmine Gideon and Elaine Unterhalter

Political Participation and Democratic Capability in Authoritarian States
Lien Pham and Ance Kaleja

The Global Architecture of Multilateral Development Banks
A System of Debt or Development?
Adrian Robert Bazbauers and Susan Engel

Philanthropic Foundations in International Development
Rockefeller, Ford and Gates
Patrick Kilby

Philanthropic Foundations in International Development
Rockefeller, Ford, and Gates

Patrick Kilby

Routledge
Taylor & Francis Group

LONDON AND NEW YORK

First published 2021
by Routledge
2 Park Square, Milton Park, Abingdon, Oxon OX14 4RN

and by Routledge
52 Vanderbilt Avenue, New York, NY 10017

Routledge is an imprint of the Taylor & Francis Group, an informa business

British Library Cataloguing in Publication Data
A catalogue record for this book is available from the British Library

Library of Congress Cataloging-in-Publication Data
Names: Kilby, Patrick, author.
Title: Philanthropic foundations in international development : Rockefeller, Ford and Gates / Patrick Kilby.
Description: Milton Park, Abingdon, Oxon ; New York, NY : Routledge, 2021. | Includes bibliographical references and index.
Identifiers: LCCN 2020052075 (print) | LCCN 2020052076 (ebook) | ISBN 9780367755409 (hardback) | ISBN 9781003162889 (ebook)
Subjects: LCSH: Charities–Developing countries. | Economic development–Developing countries.
Classification: LCC HV525 .K55 2021 (print) | LCC HV525 (ebook) | DDC 338.9109172/4–dc23
LC record available at https://lccn.loc.gov/2020052075
LC ebook record available at https://lccn.loc.gov/2020052076

ISBN: 978-0-367-75540-9 (hbk)
ISBN: 978-0-367-75542-3 (pbk)
ISBN: 978-1-003-16288-9 (ebk)

Typeset in Times New Roman
by Taylor & Francis Books

Contents

Acknowledgements

This book has helped me fill a gap in my mind, at least, as to where these household names of Rockefeller, Ford, and Gates have come from and why they are so prominent in development. For this I am most grateful to the Rockefeller Archive Center in Sleepy Hollow just outside of New York City, and its staff, in particular Tom Rosenbaum, the archivist who personally and patiently guided me through the maze of indexes and boxes of papers to examine in my few short weeks there. Finally, special thanks go to my wife, friend, and colleague Dr Joyce Wu who is a lifelong inspiration to me and provided valuable insights and input into the preparation of his book.

Preface

The late 19th-industrialist Andrew Carnegie in his paper the 'Gospel of Wealth' argued corporate philanthropy was an obligation of the very wealthy. This is mirrored 100 years later with Bill Gates' Giving Pledge, a similar call for the very wealthy to give half their wealth to philanthropic causes. These Foundations also represent what Adam Fejerskov refers to as the idea of 'private authority in global politics'. The Covid-19 pandemic and the role of the Gates' Foundation in its response is but a recent manifestation of this process. It is the sheer scale of resources that these Foundations can throw at their work that make governments pay attention. The Gates' Foundation has an endowment in the order of $50 billion, and is the second largest funder of the WHO as well as many vaccine initiatives. The Gates work follows earlier work of the Rockefeller Foundation in the 1920s and 1930s, which then was the largest funder of both its own global health programmes, and the League of Nations Health Organisation, the forerunner of the WHO. This was followed by the Ford Foundation in the 1950s and 1960s, which was very much in the Cold War mould of advancing liberal democracies and liberal education and research institutions across the developed and developing world. This book tracks the story of the very large philanthropic Foundations Rockefeller, Ford, and Gates in global development over 100 years and concludes with a discussion of the emerging foundations of the Global South, such as Ali Baba from China, which may end up having a similar role in global politics as their US forbears. The question the book explores is how 100 years of work of three foundations in particular has had a profound effect on global development in the interwar years (Rockefeller), the Cold War (Ford), and in the 21st century (Gates).

1 The foundations and philanthrocapitalism

> ... one vitally important way of bringing the dispossessed and/or alienated into the capitalist system was for robber barons (e.g., John D. Rockefeller and Andrew Carnegie) to create liberal foundations to support progressive causes like education, health care, and environmental protection schemes whose unstated hegemonic purpose was to maintain the status quo by pre-empting potentially revolutionary social change.
>
> (Barker 2008, p.17)

Introduction

The role of philanthropic foundations is often understated in contemporary global development literature, despite their role in establishing many of the well-known institutions, and funding various approaches to international development. These institutions range from the Brookings Institute in the US, Chatham House in the UK from the 1930s, to the Global Alliance for Vaccines and Immunisation (GAVI) in the 2000s. The Gates', Ford, or the Rockefeller Foundations in the US, and the Tatas and Al Waleeed in Asia, can mobilise resources on such a scale to set national and sometimes global priorities, discourse, and policy. But it is the US Foundations that have had a profound influence on international development policy and practice for the last 100 years, and continue to represent what Fejerskov refers to as 'private authority in global politics' (Fejerskov 2018, p.8). Some of these Foundations predate the post-World War II foreign aid boom by several decades, and more recently the Gates' Foundation, among others, continue this role. The global response to the COVID-19 global pandemic provides opportunities for emerging foundations from the Global South to now play a key role.

It is hard to compare figures across eras but on a GDP adjusted basis, the Ford Foundation at its peak in the mid-1960s had much the same resources available as the Bill and Melinda Gates[1] Foundation in 2000, which was in the order of $50 billion. The funding by the Rockefeller Foundation in the 1920s was probably an order of magnitude lower, but this was at a time when global investment in development work was also at a much lower level. The amount of money made available by these foundations to international development as a proportion of their total spend also varies over time. Both the Carnegie Corporation and Wellcome Trust are very large Foundations, but they spend less than 10 per cent of their total disbursements on international development, thus have less influence than, for example, the Gates' Foundation.

Of course none of this is new: the Roman Emperor Severus withdrew the rights to bequeath property to the church as its wealth had '…reached a proportion that allowed self-confident challenges to the Emperor and the state' (Fejerskov 2018, p. 48). These debates on the power and influence of Foundations and the indirect support they receive from the state in tax breaks continue in the 21st century in an era of rising nationalism. This book will keep a narrow focus on those Foundations that have been able to direct $1–2 billion annually from their endowments and are active in influencing global development policy with the Rockefeller, Ford, and Gates' Foundations used as case studies.

Global development policy here refers to the economic and social development of developing countries: issues of environmental sustainability, social equity, and national sovereignty are all critical elements in this, which give global development policy a distinctly political dimension that is heavily contested in international and other fora. This book argues as its central thesis that the Rockefeller, Ford, and Gates' Foundations have been able to shape and even dominate aspects of international development policy and practice across three eras: post-World War 1; post-World War II, and post-Cold War. They also interact in complex ways with their erstwhile partners from the Global South and sometimes, inadvertently more than deliberately, advance the interests and priorities of the Global South.

The research for this book is based on the archival records at the Rockefeller Archive Center in Tarrytown, New York State, where the Rockefeller and Ford Foundations' archives are kept. This is supplemented by a broad based literature review and contemporaneous accounts from these Foundations. This book builds on earlier research on the role of Foundations in US international relations (e.g. Parmar

2012; Berman 1983), and specifically looks at the development policy that has emerged from practice, its global dimensions, and how it was adapted by the Rockefeller and Ford Foundations in key developing countries such as China and India, as examples. This is updated with a discussion of the Gates' Foundation, which has strong similarities with, and some key differences from, Rockefeller and Ford. The book will conclude with a discussion of Foundations from the Global South, some longstanding like Tata Trusts in India from the 1880s, and more recently the very large Al Waleed Philanthropies from Saudi Arabia, and the emerging Chinese Foundations such as Ali Baba. While this book recognises the US Foundations' role in shaping domestic policy through health, education, as well as social and cultural programmes for which they are often better known, these will not be the focus, as they are covered very well elsewhere.

Philanthrocapitalism

These Foundations' legitimacy as philanthropists, comes in part from being non-profit organisations, but as Stone notes '...whether they are part of the Third Sector is more contested' (Stone 2010, p.274). The early 20th-century foundations 'had arisen in the Progressive era and their goals were consonant with the idea that human welfare was best promoted by the systematic and rational application of objective knowledge' (Kohler 1976, p.280). It was also the 'gilded age' from 1870 to 1930, a period of new technology, and the optimism it brings, but with obscene levels of wealth for some, and, increasing inequality for others, leading to social unrest. Stone argues that the period from the 1990s into the 2000s is a second gilded age (Stone 2010, p.201), with similar increases in inequality, marked by less obvious social unrest, but increased nationalism. Like Rockefeller in the first gilded age, it is Bill Gates and his influence on international health that makes the Gates' Foundation most prominent. Gates has been more clearly linked to capitalism and the private sector in health delivery, in contrast to the Rockefeller Foundation, which worked closely with public health bodies. The 21st century is also associated with the rise in what is referred to as philanthrocapitalism, which, as I argue, harks back to an earlier era.

Philanthrocapitalism in international development has become a term for what has been described as a recent phenomenon where corporations and wealthy individual engage in development activities funded by their wealth (Bishop and Green 2010; Shaw et al. 2014). These activities have been around since the early 20th century, and range from those of the traditional philanthropists to the modern version of those that engage in various social and cultural development activities. The latest iteration is in the form of social entrepreneurship and ethical sourcing and production. Any number of big name brands refer to themselves as *ethical* either in terms of fundraising for good causes as part of their operation such as for a charity causes, 'tap' a donation at point of sale, to sourcing goods ethically, or paying part of the profits back to the source country in the Global South. The other modern take on philanthrocapitalism is to use Foundations to undertake research and development activities that are about ameliorating the ill-effects of the business, or researching better ways for the business to operate. Mining companies, like BHP-Billiton, which have investments with life spans spanning several decades, have foundations funding anti-corruption, indigenous, and environmental programmes, as a way of understanding how to do business in a sustainable way in the long term.

Having a Foundation is seen to be good business as well as being philanthropic. The established foundations undertaking development work are often driven by visions of technological change, while they may directly benefit their corporate colleagues, hopefully will also make the recipients less hostile to their investments, or the associated technology. So the more recent examples of philanthrocapitalism seek to have more direct links with their own corporate goals, while staying within various regulations that often state the Foundation cannot invest in their own business. This of course is open to interpretation. While the Gates' computers in schools do not directly benefit Microsoft, the school nevertheless use Microsoft's software gifts (outside of the Foundation grant) for which the school may later pay for software updates. On the other hand Tata Trusts, which have fewer regulatory impediments, own the Tata group of companies and bring corporate social responsibility practices to their operations (Thomsen 2011).

Philanthrocapitalism can in fact be traced back to the scientific philanthropy movement of the late 19th century (McGoey 2012; Bremner 1956; Birn 2014 p.2) and the 'rags-to-riches' story of steel magnate Andrew Carnegie with his 1889 essay, 'Wealth' re-published in 1906 as the 'Gospel of Wealth', which asked the question: 'What is the proper mode of administering wealth after the laws upon which civilization is founded have thrown it into the hands of the few' (Carnegie 1889/1906, p.530). His answer was '…for the wealthy to channel their fortunes to the societal good by supporting systematic social investments rather than haphazard forms of charity' (Birn 2014, p.2). This has become a corner stone of corporate philanthropy now referred to more broadly as philanthrocapitalism, that has a direct line from Andrew Carnegie in the 19th to Bill Gates in the 21st century (Birn 2014, McGoey 2012, 2015).

Capitalism is a central component of this process of 'objective rationality', and in more recent incarnations, governments should be circumvented where possible. Or as Morvaridi puts it '...philanthropic donations support the domination of politics by the powerful and this is effectively reinforced through consensus' (2012, p.1193), and thus avoiding violent conflict. Edwards also adds that the philanthrocapitalists' belief in the efficiency of the private sector being superior to government, and so they if can raise sufficient resources for projects in the public interest, then government can be left out of the equation (Edwards 2009, p.36)

> What may be most new about philanthrocapitalism is the very explicitness of the self-interested motives underlying large-scale charitable activities...what is most notable about the new philanthropy is...less the denial or the masking of self-interest, but instead the capitalization of self-interest itself, the questionable upholding of self-interest as something indistinguishable from collective abundance.
>
> (McGoey 2012, p.197)

Carnegie's own life story came from: being a bobbin boy in a cotton factory at the age of 13; Superintendent of the Military Railways during the American civil war at the age of 26; owning his first steel company by the age of 30; and a number of other steel mills shorty after (Fejerskov 2018, p.49). This experience of early hardship may have influenced the philanthropic philosophy he pursued later in life, but not his support for the often violent conflict around the exploitation of his workers (McGoey 2012). So it was quite unusual for Carnegie as an erstwhile ruthless 'robber baron', to support inheritance taxes (Carnegie (1889)1906), which he saw as:

> An antidote for the temporary unequal distribution of wealth ... differing, indeed, from that of the Communist in requiring only the further evolution of existing conditions, not the total overthrow of our civilization.
>
> (p.533)

Other Foundations such as Ford had a sharply different view on inheritance taxes, and were set up to specifically avoid them. The approach Carnegie adopted was based on the philosophy of *scientific philanthropy* '... of preventing rather than of relieving distress' (Bremner 1956, p.173). The first decades of the 20th century also marked an end of an 'era of accumulation' of the 19th century '... and its replacement by a "century of redistribution" a task which itself became big business' (Bell 2000, p.484). These philosophic ideals set the scene and norms for philanthropy through the 20th and into the 21st century, guiding the work of the Rockefeller, Gates and Ford Foundations. While the philosophy of the scientific philanthropism was to recognise the role of the state, and to influence its agenda and support it (Arnove and Pined 2007), most philanthropic foundations at heart, are also about preserving the *status quo* of liberal capitalism, and that is certainly the case for the 21st century incarnations of the modern Foundation.

> Despite their more progressive, if not radical, rhetoric and approaches to community building that give voice to those who have been disadvantaged by the workings of an increasingly global capitalist economy, they [Foundations] remain ultimately elitist and technocratic institutions.
>
> (Arnove and Pined 2007, p. 422)

The 21st-century version of scientific philanthropy is very much tied to the ideas of neo-liberalism. This is what sets it apart from the earlier 20th-century Foundations: a scepticism of the role of the state and seeking to diminish it, if not to replace it, with more market-based mechanisms. The effect of this, shown in Chapter 4 on the Gates' Foundation is, despite the rhetoric, a shift of emphasis away from reaching the poor in society. This shift is simply because it is easier to reach the less poor members of society who are more embedded in the market, and they are more able to provide an economic return on investment.

Carnegie's support of ideas of objective rationality and *scientific philanthropy* have been long debated and is a theme of this book. Most Foundations, however, are based on more varied motivations, such as religious obligations as was the case with the John D Rockefeller and his philanthropic work, guided by the Reverend Frederick Gates, of the late 19th and early 20th century, and Indian Parsees for the Tata Trusts from the 1890s (Worden 2003). More prosaically, another and not insignificant motivation, was gaining a business advantage, or skirting tax obligations as was the case with the Ford Foundation in its pre-war years, and the IKEA Foundation post-war.

It was when the Ford and Rockefeller Foundations moved to the hands of their grandsons, John D Rockefeller III and Henry Ford II, after the Second World War, that a more liberal view of the world took hold. In the case of the Gates' Foundation, like the early Rockefeller Foundation years, it was Bill Gates' ardent belief in the role of technology in addressing social problems, whether it be health or education, that drove the work. Overlaying these motives, particularly through the 20th century, was a widely held view that the primary driver of the Foundations was to cement the central role of capitalism and a liberal world view. This was not only in theory but also in practice in terms of their role in various national policies across the Global South, as well as a being a driver for business opportunities for themselves and their colleagues (McGoey 2015; Fejerskov 2018). This interlinking web of motivations will be the focus of this book.

Philanthropic foundations and US foreign policy

There is little doubt that the Rockefeller Foundation shaped the US in its interwar foreign policy, despite the scepticism of the US Congress and many in the US administration of the Foundation's legitimacy in its early years. The Ford Foundation played an important role in shaping the US post-World War II foreign aid and international policy, and the Gates' Foundation continued this policy work, particularly in health, in the 21st century. The Foundations did this not only through their own aid programs, for example, in health and education, but in their support for academic research to guide government policy through funding research and establishing think tanks for what they felt was important and relevant, and supported their world view. These influential think tanks included Brookings and IFPRI in the US, and Chatham House and ODI in the UK, have been all leaders in influencing the West's global aid and development agenda, at least until the early 21st century when China and others have started to provide clear competition in both scale, scope, and ideology. The US in the late 2010s under the Trump administration was more inward looking and nationalist, and less inclined to these liberal influences, but this is not new. Liberalism has been under direct challenge by various illiberal turns from the McCarthy era attacks on the Ford Foundation in the 1950s, to contemporary attacks by Trump on the Gates' Foundation, or from foreign governments on both George Soros's Open Society Foundation and the Ford Foundation. The Biden administration has shifted on these views, but to what extent remains an open question,

It was not only the foreign aid programmes of countries like the US that the Foundations helped to shape, but also the UN and its agencies. The post-war World Health Organization's (WHO) programme was shaped not only by the Rockefeller Foundation's support to its predecessor the League of Nations Health Organisation (LNHO) in the 1920s and 1930s, but it also more or less followed the Rockefeller Foundation's own health programme's organisational structure (Tournès 2014). The WHO continues to be shaped most recently by the Gates' Foundation support, particularly after the 2020 US withdrawal from WHO under Trump (later overturned by Biden in 2021), 100 years after the Rockefeller Foundation support for the LNHO, also in the absence of US membership and support at the time (Clarke 2019). To a lesser extent it can be argued that the Food and Agriculture Organisation (FAO), UNHCR, UNRAA, and other programmes, and their antecedents have all been influenced by the support of the major US foundations, and in the case of IFAD, the Aga Khan Foundation. International organisations such as IFPRI, and the network of CGIAR agricultural research institutes led by IRRI and CYMMIT, all were established by either the Ford or Rockefeller Foundations, or both, and have their continued patronage.

These Foundations not only provided foreign aid, in and of themselves, but they also have inter-penetrated government policy-making in both the Global North and South to a remarkable degree and shaped both inter-war and post-World War II development policy and practice. This was often driven by a technocratic approach to solving human development problems. This not only provided opportunities for US capital to invest, but also pushed the broader ideology of modernisation and liberal democracy. Technical advances, at least in the early years of the Rockefeller and Ford Foundations, and now with Gates' were, and still are, seen as the answer to social problems such as health and hunger (McGoey 2015; Fejerskov 2018).

This ideological focus enabled the Foundations to side-step local politics and politicians as much as possible. In doing so they also overlooked the voice of the local recipients, and their communities who were largely absent in this work with a few important exceptions: including the LNHO public health work in East Asia between the wars; the Ford Foundation's close relationship with the Indian government and its National Planning Office; as well as Ford's community development work in India and elsewhere in the 1950s, all of which this book will explore.

The role of Foundations in shaping global policy raises the question of the role of elites, and what Berman refers to as elite governance, and an American led global hegemony (Berman 1983). Of course there are no shortages of examples where Foundation support was used, knowingly or unknowingly, to counter this hegemony, such as the Rockefeller Foundation in China in the inter-war years, or Ford in India post-World War II (Sackley 2012), both of which will be returned to in Chapters Two and Three of this volume. Whether these Foundations were as hegemonic as some writers argue is open for debate, but certainly they were driven by what Mike Edwards refers to as an East Coast (US) liberal tradition of reform not transformation, to defend capitalism, and at best, seek to reform it (Edwards 2019). McGoey (2012, 2015) argues that this exercise of quasi-corporate power is overreach and a threat to existing national and international institutions. This book argues that while this has been true since Rockefeller and Carnegie, Foundations have also been important players in the development landscape, and both local and international levels. The question remaining, however, is the extent to which the more local positive contributions are overshadowed by McGoey's argument of corporate overreach.

This book will explore the role of the Foundations in the US and Western development policy establishment through three major Foundations: the Rockefeller, Ford, and Gates' as case studies. The book will conclude with discussion of the future and the emergence of Foundations of from the Global South such as the newer Al Waleed Philanthropies and the long standing Tata Trusts. It will also look at the emerging Foundations from China and elsewhere, such as Ali Baba, and how they may seek to shape global development policy in a post-COVID world.

There will be a strong US focus as that is where the most influential Foundations have been located, and where their influence has built up over the longest period. Both Rockefeller and Carnegie first made their mark in the latter half of the 19th and the first half of the 20th century, Ford the latter half of the 20th century, and Gates' and Open Society in the 21st century (Parmar 2012; Roelofs 2007). This represents well over 100 years of a profound influence in the processes of international development from its nascent years post-World War I, to being major players in Presidents Truman and Kennedy's post-World War II visions of development. The 2010s has seen a post-Cold War fracturing of earlier alliances, with the more recent rise of nationalism, the Global South, and the closely related challenges to US hegemony, helped to some extent by former US President Trump's move from internationalism and international leadership to a more inward focus, driven in part by the COVID-19 pandemic.

Foundations and the global policy establishment

From the 1920s there were two parallel movements: the first was a dangerous isolationism in the US, in the period of post-World War I uncertainty (Williams 1954; Mariano 2011); and the second movement, by way of contrast, was a nascent internationalism through the League of Nations (LoN) (Tournès 2014). This inter-war period was also at a time of festering resentment from some of the major powers in how they were treated at the Versailles Peace Conference and associated processes, most notably Germany, Japan, and China (Brooks 1992). To counter the US isolationism and rejection of the LoN, and support the internationalism, the major Foundations of the time, Rockefeller and Carnegie

... helped construct the hegemony of liberal internationalism, marginalized isolationism, and built up the institutional capacities of the [US] federal government, especially in foreign affairs.

(Parmar 2012, p.3)

They did this through a process of strategic support and funding, as well as targeted patronage to provide '... the domestic intellectual and political bases that would assist America's rise to global leadership' (p.2), and to this could be added international networks and institutions in the production of knowledge that had a clear liberal slant. While they were unable to affect the outcome of the post-war settlement of the Versailles Conference of 1919 and its aftermath, which was to be another major war 20 years later, the Foundations were able to lay the base for the rise of the US globally over the 50 years post-World War II. The Carnegie Corporation was to do this through domestic policy work (Johnstone 2014), while the Rockefeller Foundation also had a substantial international focus, that included work in nascent developing countries in Africa and Asia, then colonies of the mainly European powers.

Rockefeller, in particular, did this in the inter-war years through large-scale funding in particular areas to drive research and mainstream policy thinking. While there were clear practical gains in health and agriculture, their main aim was to cultivate cultural and intellectual elites in the US, Europe, and the nascent Global South who would take on leadership roles in inter-war processes and fora. This strategy was not entirely successful as these elites did not necessarily follow the liberal democratic mould the Foundations preferred (Scott-Smith 2014). This was in part due to the ideological positions of those concerned (an Atlantic divide) between Europe and the US, the lack of relevance of many of the liberal arguments being promoted, but also that many European institutions had a more pluralist approach to training their own and Third World elites, tending to resist US hegemony in higher education, and the ideological directions it suggested.

Prior to World War II the training of those elites was mainly in Europe while post-World War II there was a marked shift to the newly emerging independent developing countries. This, however, was not as clear cut with the Rockefeller Foundation including developing country scholars in its exchange programme from the 1920s, and much of its work in China during the inter-war period was at the elite education level. Carnegie was more limited in scope and mainly focussed in the US, but did some education work in British colonial Africa in support of the Empire in the 1920s and 1930s.

The driving motivation of these Foundations was based on the: 'Wilsonian conviction that the United States had a responsibility to enhance the welfare of those living beyond its borders' (Shepherd 2005, p.116). This in turn had its origins in the early years of the Republic and Jeffersonian ideals:

> Trusted with the destinies of this solitary republic of the world, the only monument of human rights, and the sole depository of the sacred fire of freedom and self-government, from hence it is to be lighted up in other regions of the earth, if other areas of the earth shall ever become susceptible of its benign influence.
>
> Thomas Jefferson on leaving the Presidency 1809 quoted in (Tucker and Hendrickson 1990, p.7)

Thus the Foundations and their work became an integral part of what was to become known as 'American exceptionalism', the belief that the US had a near divine mandate to spread its liberal democratic values across the globe, while at the same time taking advantage of business opportunities as they arose: '... an American imperium a hegemony constructed in significant part via cultural and intellectual penetration' (Parmar 2012, p.2). To a large extent it was the major US Foundations that enabled that to happen, but it was also this American exceptionalism that gave rise to a resentment that developed in the post-colonial world of international development. There was a perception by developing countries of the West in general, and the US in particular, of a neo-colonial 'turn', with the major Foundation being a focus of this resentment, something that has persisted well into the 21st century. Both Ford and the Open Society Foundations have been 'put on notice' if not outright banned in many developing countries (Mallet 2015; Clarke 2019).

The Rockefeller Foundation probably exemplified American exceptionalism, particularly in its early years, the Ford Foundation post-World War II, and the Gates' and Open Society Foundations post-Cold War. The influence of these Foundations is directly related to the vast wealth their founders amassed to be able to influence global outcomes. In the cases of Rockefeller and Ford it was not the founders' vision *per se* that drove the Foundation on to the global stage, but that of their sons or in the case of Ford the grandson, who made these two Foundations the behemoths they were to become. While it might be presumptuous to speculate why the heirs took such an active role in the Foundations, one reason might be: to make better use of the 'ill-gotten gains' of the founders.

In the case of Rockefeller, the wealth was from oil; Carnegie, steel; Ford, the motor car; Gates computer software; and Soros, currency speculation and hedge funds. Each was able to change the very way their businesses functioned to create near monopolies, and change the world to an image that suited their world view. John D. Rockefeller with Standard Oil and Andrew Carnegie with Carnegie Steel had a single minded ruthlessness and were referred to as 'robber barons', receiving trenchant criticism by both the broader community, and the policy establishment of the time (Barker 2008; Roelofs 2003; Nielsen 1972). Henry Ford and his son Edsel avoided the moniker of being 'robber barons' but, similar to Rockefeller and Carnegie, they were single-minded in dominating the US car industry, and used the family Foundation and its holding of the company stock, as a strategy in defeating business rivals and avoiding inheritance tax. Bill Gates was sued for anti-trust activities just prior to the Foundation being launched, and Soros' currency gambles collapsed currencies and with that local economies (Clarke 2019).

In the case of the Ford and Rockefeller Foundations, which moved to an active international development focus, it was John D. Rockefeller II, and Henry Ford II who inherited the family businesses and the associated Foundations and took a more active interest in them. They saw it as a way of shaping the US socially and economically, and for Rockefeller and Carnegie, the post-Civil War legacy of sharp racial and social divisions within the US that were hard to shake off, provided important opportunities for both Foundations, and from these they moved to have a global stage.

This 'shaping' was at first tentative with an eye to public opinion, as Rockefeller and Carnegie were both very much in the Congressional and public eye. There were two elements that guided them: first, was the technological driven economic boom from the 1870s (the 'gilded' age) that created the enormous wealth for both Rockefeller and Carnegie; and second, was the fundamental class and racial cleavages in US society that this boom, together with the largely unjust post-Civil War settlement, brought. At times this cleavage threatened the very fabric of society in some places, particularly in the South (Parmar 2012; Mitchell and Lowe 1990).

The Rockefeller and Carnegie Foundations in the early 20th century, and Ford from the 1950s, adopted what was essentially a two-pronged approach: programmes that focussed on disadvantage but carefully avoided addressing the structural issues that created that disadvantage; and second, through programmes to influence public thinking and knowledge production, through the support of Universities and think tanks. Rockefeller started this process with the re-creation of the University of Chicago from a small church based Chicago college, run by the American Baptist Education Society in the 1880s. The University of Chicago was to go onto produce 98 Nobel laureates, the most for any University, and challenge the Ivy League for prestige. Almost all of the well-known Universities and public think tanks in the US, and many elsewhere, can thank the Foundations either for their coming into being, or the beneficiary of generous grants to build key schools and faculties to steer the direction of research.

In the first half of the 20th century the focus was on the pure sciences through Rockefeller, and in the second half, it was more on the social sciences and arts both at home and abroad through the Ford Foundation. While this to a certain extent is an oversimplification, the argument has more than a grain of truth. The science focus arguably led to the Green Revolution, and the social sciences work led to the post-war development boom, and the rapid expansion of area studies and international development programs across elite US universities.

Up until the 1920s, the prevailing social and racial tensions in the US led the Foundations to focus on ameliorating them lest these turn into more dangerous political movements, even if this Foundation work was to reinforce existing class and racial hierarchies. Education and other services to reach poor and marginalised groups initially in the US, focusing on the South, was then extended abroad (Mitchell and Lowe 1990; Berman 1983). From 1920 to the 1940s the Foundations' work was to deal with the aftermath of World War I, and its own social and political legacy, including US isolationism, and the social and economic restructuring that followed, as well as seeking to address the global threats from those countries left out of the post-World War I settlement, in particular China, Japan, and Germany. Again, a dual approach was taken with programmes mainly in health as well as steering knowledge production, with a focus on the technical and biological sciences. This was also a period of tentative forays into what would be called foreign aid, largely in the health sector in Asia, and education in Africa, but importantly, some tentative steps in agriculture and food production.

After World War II, the Cold War drove much thinking and programmes to support decolonisation and the associated economic and social development of the emerging powers. It was important for the liberal Foundations that the US rather than the Soviet Union or China, was the source of support for these emerging powers' development. At the same time the post-War boom had to be harnessed intellectually, to challenge the emerging McCarthyite anti-communist isolationism. Similar to the inter-war period, post-World War II there was investment both in education and higher learning to expand the liberal world view of US students and scholars, and to train emerging leaders from the Global South. Social programmes were established to lead to a form of social engineering that looked at alleviating some of the symptoms of some of the more unjust social and political structures: in the international development field, the Foundations' work, like US Cold War policy, was strategic and focussed on what Berman called the 'underbelly of China' (Berman 1983, p.56). This was also a period of intense scrutiny of the Foundations, as the Ford Foundation had entered the scene eclipsing its rivals by the sheer scale of the financial resources it had available.

Like the scrutiny the Rockefeller Foundation was subject to in the early 1900s from the left of the political spectrum, accusing it of being anti-worker, post-World War II it was a right-wing McCarthyite gaze that settled on the Foundations. It accused them of funding left-wing and communist causes, not least of which were civil rights and left leaning governments, such as that of Jawaharlal Nehru in India. Internationally, the Foundations have been accused of being CIA agents, or in the case of George Soros and the Open Society Foundations, promoting a Western form of liberalism. The Foundations have managed to attract flak from both the left and the right as their promotion of a liberal world order to enable capitalism to thrive, was challenged by the sharper ideological positions of the Marxist left, on the one hand and the conservative right on the other, both of which preferred their respective illiberal views.

By the turn of the 21st century these ideological battles seemed to be over with a neo-liberal consensus emerging, in the US at least. When the Gates' Foundation came on the scene it had a relatively easy ride in terms of public scrutiny. While the Microsoft Corporation came under fire for anti-trust activities similar to the 'robber barons' of yesteryear, the hostility was not as deeply rooted in society as it affected workers' pay packets much less. As a result, the level of scrutiny did not spill over into the associated Foundation in the same way. Like its Rockefeller predecessor 100 years before, the Gates' Foundation has had a profound influence in medical research. The search for the nirvana of disease eradication through technology in the form of (sometimes expensive) universal vaccination, like Rockefeller and yellow fever eradication before it, Gates' has had a series of setbacks in vaccine development and roll out, with no major breakthroughs to date. These experiences beg the question of the very idea of eradicating diseases, rather than managing them. Also like Rockefeller, for Gates' the goal of disease eradication is at the expense of public health, but the scale of the funding seems to be enough to stifle most criticism. The COVID-19 pandemic of the 2020s and the necessary public health response is a clear challenge to those views.

Conclusion

The challenge the philanthropic Foundations create is that it is hard to categorise them beyond bland statements of them on the one hand supporting liberal causes, or technocratic approaches to problem solving, neither of which alone is problematic; or on the other hand being part of western hegemonic and corporate processes. The issue is not really about these competing arguments, but it is about the resources that Foundations can throw at particular problem that are so large they can skew any broader contest of ideas with respect to a particular problem. The Rockefeller, Ford, and Gates' Foundations have at various times in their existence been able to not only shape the direction of policy and broader thinking on international development, to reflect what could be called East Coast (US) liberal values, but to also change practice and the associated international institutes such as WHO, and in some cases fund their establishment such as GAVI, AGRA, and the CGIAR network of agricultural research institutes, and then pressure governments and donors to pick up the slack.

While there is not a lot that the international community can do about this given the lifeline that Foundation funding can provide, it does give cause for concern on how global consensus is reached on some of these decision and how it can be 'bought' to reflect the whims of very rich benefactors. It also raises the issue of the narrowing of the contest of ideas, or indeed steering the direction of debate. In the 1920s and 1930s there was an undercurrent of racism in some of the Foundations' work: the secondary education programmes of Carnegie, focussed on vocational education for black students rather than general education in the US and Southern Africa; and the Rockefeller Foundation funded eugenic related research in Germany and the US (Levine 2010; Weindling 1985). In the 1950s onwards the Ford Foundation had a profound influence in political science research and international studies on how international development should be seen. There was little funding available for researching the increased roles of the state and Keynesian economics, let alone socialist political science, or political economy. Likewise Gates' has little interest in public health solutions to complex diseases.

Note

1 I later use Gates' as a plural shorthand.

References

Arnove, Robert, and Nadine Pined. 2007. 'Revisiting the "Big Three" Foundations.' *Critical Sociology* 33 (33).

Barker, Michael 2008. 'The Liberal Foundations of Environmentalism: Revisiting the Rockefeller-Ford Connection.' *Capitalism Nature Socialism* 19 (2):15–42.

Bell, Morag. 2000. 'American Philanthropy, the Carnegie Corporation and Poverty in South Africa.' *Journal of Southern African Studies* 26 (3): 481–504.

Berman, Edward H. 1983. *The influence of the Carnegie, Ford, and Rockefeller Foundations on American foreign policy: The ideology of philanthropy.* Albany, NY: SUNY Press.

Birn, Anne-Emanuelle. 2014. 'Philanthrocapitalism, Past and Present: The Rockefeller Foundation, the Gates Foundation, and the Setting (s) of the International/Global Health Agenda.' *Hypothesis* 12 (1): e8.

Bishop, Mathew, and Michael Green. 2010. *Philanthrocapitalism: How Giving Can Save the World.* New York: Bloomsbury.

Bremner, Robert H. 1956.'"Scientific Philanthropy, 1873–93.' *Social Service Review* 30 (2): 168–173.

Brooks, Jeffrey. 1992. 'Official Xenophobia and Popular Cosmopolitanism in Early Soviet Russia.' *The American Historical Review* 97 (5): 1431–1448.

Carnegie, Andrew. (1889)1906. 'The Gospel of Wealth.' *North American Review* 183 (599): 526–537.

Clarke, Gerard. 2019. 'The New Global Governors: Globalization, Civil Society, and the Rise of Private Philanthropic Foundations.' *Journal of Civil Society* 15 (3): 197–213.

Edwards, Michael. 2009. 'Gates, Google, and the Ending of Global Poverty: Philanthrocapitalism and International Development.' *The Brown Journal of World Affairs* 15 (2): 35–42.

Edwards, Michael. 2019. Interview Sept 26.

Fejerskov, Adam Moe. 2018. *The Gates Foundation's Rise to Power: Private Authority in Global Politics*. Abingdon: Routledge.

Johnstone, Andrew. 2014. "'Shaping Our Post-War Foreign Policy: The Carnegie Endowment for International Peace and the Promotion of the United Nations Organisation during World War II.' *Global Society* 28 (1): 24–39. https://doi.org/10.1080/13600826.2013.848185.

Kohler, Robert E. 1976. 'The management of science: The experience of Warren Weaver and the Rockefeller Foundation programme in molecular biology.' *Minerva* 14 (3): 279–306.

Levine, Philippa. 2010. 'Anthropology, Colonialism, and Eugenics.' In Alison Bashford and Philippa Levine (eds) *The Oxford Handbook of the History of Eugenics*, 43–61. New York: Oxford University Press.

Mallet, Victor. 2015. 'India Targets Ford Foundation as National Security Risk.' *Financial Times*.

Mariano, Marco. 2011. 'Isolationism, internationalism and the Monroe Doctrine.' *Journal of Transatlantic Studies* 9 (1): 35–45.

McGoey, Linsey. 2012. 'Philanthrocapitalism and Its Critics.' *Poetics* 40 (2): 185–199.

McGoey, Linsey. 2015. *No Such Thing as a Free Gift: The Gates Foundation and the Price of Philanthropy*. London: Verso Books.

Mitchell, Theodore R., and Robert Lowe. 1990. 'To sow contentment: Philanthropy, scientific agriculture and the making of the new South: 1906–1920.' *Journal of Social History* 24 (2): 317–340.

Morvaridi, Behrooz. 2012. 'Capitalist Philanthropy and Hegemonic Partnerships.' *Third World Quarterly* 33 (7): 1191–1210. https://doi.org/10.1080/01436597.2012.691827.

Nielsen, Waldemar A. 1972. *The Big Foundations*. New York: Columbia University Press.

Parmar, Inderjeet. 2012. *Foundations of the American Century: The Ford, Carnegie, and Rockefeller Foundations in the Rise of American Power*. New York: Columbia University Press.

Roelofs, Joan. 2003. *Foundations and public policy: The mask of pluralism*. Albany: SUNY Press.

Roelofs, Joan. 2007. 'Foundations and collaboration.' *Critical Sociology* 33 (3): 479–504.

Sackley, Nicole. 2012. 'Foundation in the Field: The Ford Foundation New Delhi Office and the Construction of Development Knowledge, 1951–1970.'" In *University of Richmond UR Scholarship Repository-History*. Richmond, VA: University of Richmond.

Scott-Smith, Giles. 2014. 'Maintaining Transatlantic Community: US Public Diplomacy, the Ford Foundation and the Successor Generation Concept in US Foreign Affairs, 1960s–1980s.' *Global Society* 28 (1): 90–103.

Shaw, Ealanor, Jillian Gordon, MairiMaclean, and Charles Harvey. 2014. 'Venture and Philanthrocapitalism: The Impact of the Big Donor.' In *The Routledge Companion to Philanthropy*. Abingdon: Routledge.

Shepherd, Chris J. 2005. 'Imperial science: The Rockefeller Foundation and Agricultural Science in Peru, 1940–1960.' *Science as Culture* 14 (2): 113–137.

Stone, Diane. 2010. 'Private Philanthropy or Policy Transfer? The Transnational Norms of the Open Society Institute'. *Policy & Politics* 38 (2): 269–287.

Thomsen, Steen. 2011. 'Trust Ownership of the Tata Group.' SSRN 1976958. Center for Corporate Governance, Copenhagen Business School.

Tournès, Ludovic. 2014. 'The Rockefeller Foundation and the Transition from the League of Nations to the UN (1939–1946).' *Journal of Modern European History* 12 (3): 323–341.

Tucker, Robert W., and David C.Hendrickson. 1990. *Empire of liberty: The statecraft of Thomas Jefferson*. New York: Oxford University Press.

Weindling, Paul. 1985. '"Weimar Eugenics": The Kaiser Wilhelm Institute for Anthropology, Human Heredity and Eugenics in Social Context.' *Annals of Science* 42 (3): 303–318.

Williams, William Appleman. 1954. 'The Legend of Isolationism in the 1920s.' *Science & Society* 1954: 1–20.

Worden, Skip. 2003. 'The Role of Religious and Nationalist Ethics in Strategic Leadership: The Case of JN Tata.' *Journal of Business Ethics* 47 (2): 147–164.

2   The Rockefeller Foundation

This sense of working 'backward to the present' was a cardinal feature of Rockefeller sponsored modernisation. By designing the future reformers believed they could vanquish hunger and poverty, birthing a new world that aligned more clearly with US strategic interests.

(Nally and Taylor 2015, p.22)

Introduction

The Rockefeller Foundation is probably the largest and most well-known of the early 20th-Century Foundations. Making an estimate of the relative scale of the Rockefeller Foundation's funding to that of more contemporary Foundations is difficult, as accounting for inflation and the like does not take into account respective sizes of the economy. If we use a GDP measure to account for the increasing size of the US economy over time, then the original $180 million of grants in 1909 and 1920, GDP adjusted, would be around $18 billion in 2000 dollars. This compares with Ford at its peak in the mid 1960s of $45 billion and Gates at $50 billion. But in the 1920s the global interest and involvement in foreign aid was much lower so the Foundation's impact was much greater. The Rockefeller Foundation was the largest single international development actor until the 1940s, spending more on development than any state, international organisation, or NGO (Fejerskov 2015 p.56). Until the advent of the World Health Organization (WHO) in 1948 the Rockefeller Foundation's International Health Division (IHD) was arguably the most important agency in global health work. Its annual grants in the 1920s and 1930s were of the order of $2–3 billion in 2020 GDP adjusted dollars (Youde 2013, p.143).

This chapter argues that the Rockefeller Foundation shaped international development policy and practice almost alone in terms of

Foundation influence from the 1920s until the 1950s. It also had a role in influencing governments of the Global South and inadvertently, nascent independence movements. More importantly the Rockefeller Foundation at the local level at least, was also shaped by these local actors. This relationship was complex, contradictory, and very much context specific. While the Foundation leadership in New York in the 1920s and 1930s took a white male view of the world, going so far as attempting to shape society through funding eugenics programmes including those in Germany in the 1930s, the field offices were building local partnerships in China and Asia more broadly, before the war, and in places like India and Mexico after the war under the more liberal leadership of the founder's grandson John D Rockefeller III.

The early years

The Rockefeller Foundation was formally constituted in 1913, from an idea that emerged in 1901 when the oil magnate John D. Rockefeller first considered setting up a very large Foundation with his vast oil wealth. This followed two decades of Rockefeller philanthropy within the US with the Rev Frederick Gates as his confidant and adviser: setting up the University of Chicago in 1892; the Rockefeller Institute for Medical Research in 1901; and the General Education Board in 1903 (Fosdick 1952). While these were quite substantial, they were seen by Rockefeller and Gates as still relatively small investments. But they were a model to enable them to bring their philanthropy on to a global stage. The Institute of Medical Research provided the model for the Foundation's International Health Commission (IHC), and General Education Board for its later research on agricultural development. Frederick Gates believed that 'if science and education are the brains and nervous system of civilisation, health is its heart' (Fejerskov 2018, p.52).

It was not until 1906 that a model for the Foundation was developed in some detail. In a 1905 note to John D. Rockefeller, Frederick Gates, clearly inspired by close friend and colleague Andrew Carnegie's 1889's paper the 'Gospel of Wealth' (Carnegie 1889/1906), wrote:

> The moral responsibility of discharging this vast trust fully ... is with inexorable logic also your own. It must be delegated to the unborn and unknown or it must be discharged by you. It seems to me that it must not, it ought not, it cannot be rightfully delegated to the unknown and the unknowable.
>
> (Gates 1905a, p.2)

In the same note he suggested by way of example a global health fund (p.4), as well as a strong preference for support to Protestants and the British Empire '...we should leave Catholicism like Mohammedanism to the slow progress of geological time [and] let us work with and for the British Empire' (Gates 1905b, pp.3,7).

Some have suggested the establishment of a Foundation was an attempt to 'whitewash' the image of the Rockefeller family following very bad press and a book very critical of Standard Oil (Tarbell 1904), as well as the belief the family fortune would be dissipated by the children (Chernow 1988). John D. Rockefeller's existing philanthropic work since the 1880s gives lie to that suggestion. However, this was a period when the Rockefeller family, and Standard Oil in particular, was at the centre of a number of scandals. There was a large fine imposed (later overturned) for ant-trust activities (Nielsen 1972); and in 1911 the US Supreme Court found Standard Oil in violation of the Sherman Anti-trust Act and it was broken up into 34 separate com-panies (Fosdick 1952; Yergin 1991). This fed the not unreasonable narrative of the time, which still continues, that it is the working poor who are the real philanthropists by virtue of the opportunity costs of their low wages (Ehrenreich 2010), and in the popular press, these working poor were referred to as the 'unwilling philanthropists' (Lippincott 1913).

Having a new and much larger Foundation in the Rockefeller name was a timely initiative in a time of public and congressional hostility. It was also at the time referred to as both the 'gilded age' of excess (1870–1930), and the Progressive era (1890s to 1920s) in which there was a strong social movement for economic reform including stronger corporate regulation to counter the robber barons. Rockefeller and Carnegie as the leading 'robber barons' of that era felt they had to respond through their Foundation work and by giving away much of their fortune. Nevertheless, the public hostility to the Rockefellers (father and son) and their business interests remained undiminished and led to delays of Federal registration by the US Congress, which called the nascent Foundation 'a menace to national welfare' (Trenton Evening Times 1915; Hinricks 1923). The obvious links the Rock-efeller Foundation had with Standard Oil, and the poor reputation it had, gave plenty of ammunition for closer scrutiny (Fosdick 1952, Parmar 2012). The central issue for the US Congress was:

> ... whether there was a dividing line between Mr. Rockefeller's interests and the interests of the Rockefeller Foundation the result

was the Foundation must become primarily not an operating agency but a fund dispensing agency.

(Fosdick 1952, pp.26–27)

Thus, the initial focus of the Foundation was to be a funding agency to other institutions, and it was not until the agricultural work in Mexico in 1943 that it became an operational agency in its own right, undertaking its own programmes directly. The federal registration process dragged on for three years, and ultimately Congress prevented it from being federally registered. The Foundation, however, was able to be registered as a Trust in New York State in 1913. Its reputation continued to be tarnished with subsequent events such John D. Rockefeller II's involvement in the 1914 Ludlow massacre of striking coal miners by the National Guard, and the subsequent Colorado Coalfield War (Clarke 2019, p.202).

The first steps in setting up the Foundation was in 1909 when John D. Rockefeller signed over 73,000 Standard Oil shares valued at $50 million to a Trust with the three inaugural trustees: his son John D. Rockefeller II; his son-in-law Harold Fowler McCormick; and the Rev Frederick Gates. This was the first instalment of a projected $180 million endowment with the remainder paid in 1914 following formal registration ($50 milliom) and in 1922 ($80 million) (Rockefeller Foundation 1914, 1922). The objects of the Foundation were:

> ... to promote the well-being and to advance the civilisation of the peoples of the United States and its territories and possessions and of foreign lands in the acquisition and dissemination of knowledge, in the prevention and relief of suffering, and in the promotion of any and all the elements of human progress.

(Farley 2004, p.3)

This moved the work of the Rockefellers' philanthropic work onto the world stage and the field of international development well before governments, international agencies, and most NGOs became involved. The first programme of the Foundation was the elimination of hookworm in the British colonies, followed by the elimination of yellow fever starting in Latin America (Rockefeller Foundation 1915, 1916, 1918, 1921).

The Rockefellers and their Foundation soon moved away from the confines of the British Empire and the Protestant Christian focus of Rev Gates' 'vision', but it continued to have a strong belief that 'human welfare was best promoted by the systemic and rational application of objective knowledge' (Kohler 1976, p.280). The Foundation was also linked to US diplomacy, with its style of paternalism tied to US economic expansion (Shepherd 2005). The agenda to relieve global social tensions also took a hold in the Foundation, and grew over the following 50 years, based on Carnegie's idea that:

> ... massive concentrated wealth, if administered unwisely, might inspire dangerous and destabilizing class tensions ... [and to this was later added] fears of population growth, dwindling resources, peasant insurgency and communism.
>
> (Nally 2015, p.52)

These mixed motives inevitably led to tensions between the harder line technocrats in leadership, US diplomats, and the on-ground programme people within the Foundation. This was to play out over the following 100 years as the influence of each of these groups waxed and waned, but as far as the head office was concerned, at least up until the World War II:

> ... the RF's singular focus on the objects of knowledge – seed, plants, pathogens and yields among others – enabled attention to be consistently diverted from social and political phenomena toward supposedly neutral objects of knowledge.
>
> (Jennings 1988, p.27)

Despite these lofty goals many compromises were made in the Foundation's approach to the wider world and associated political field to ensure its broader influence, most evident in its health and agriculture work, more often than not in opposition to the Head Office vision. The public health work of the IHD, for example, was broad-based and on a very large scale. Warren Weaver as Director of the Division of Natural Sciences from 1932 to 1955 was trenchantly opposed to applied research, and was in constant tension with the Trustees on one hand and the field staff on the other, who both sought more applied approaches to sciences funding, to deal with the common real world issues such as agricultural productivity and public health.

The slow communications with the field at the time, and the widely spread programme probably weakened Weaver's authority in the field. But he still argued that: 'The real program in biology depends upon the importance to man [sic] that he understands himself ... this aim transcends all of the practical arguments for biological research' (Weaver 1942a, p.1). Even when agriculture was identified by the trustees as a focus in the 1930s it was not until 1942 and the exigencies of war that Weaver relented, noting:

> I feel confident that at least some of the trustees will think that we are unrealistic impractical and that we are living in an academic ivory tower [however] ... the Rockefeller Foundation cannot possibly afford to disregard some of the important emergency opportunities which will appear.
>
> (Weaver 1942b, p.1)

From the 1950s on the Foundation continued to broaden its work beyond the scientific, which we will return to later, however, the next section will focus on the first half of the 20th century and look at the most important focus for the Foundation in its international work at the time: health.

Health

The initial work of the Rockefeller Foundation focussed on health and disease eradication through first, the Institute for Medical Research established in 1901 and the Rockefeller Sanitary Commission (RSC) in 1909, which through a series of restructures and re-namings became the International Health Division (IHD) in 1928.[1] The RSC had focussed on eradicating hookworm through a public health campaign across the South of the US, before going international:

> ... [it] showered eleven southern states with teams of physicians, sanitary inspectors, and laboratory technicians who administered deworming medication; promoted shoe wearing and latrine use; and disseminated public health materials, working through churches and agricultural clubs.
>
> (Birn and Richter 2017, pp.10–15)

This early work highlighted the differences within the Foundation between technical and social approaches to problems solving. The RSC took a public health approach, through an education campaign to eradicate hookworm and later yellow fever from 1915 to 1925. It was successful to the point that by 1925 only three cases of yellow fever were found in all of the Americas (Rockefeller Foundation 1925, p.17). But of course, neither yellow fever nor hookworm were eradicated and continue to be global public health problems.

Later the work of the IHD took on a more technical approach to disease control. For example, part of the yellow fever work involved the development of a vaccine that was successful in Brazil in 1939, and is still in use globally (Nielsen 1972; World Health Organization 2013). However, the Foundation also had its setbacks including developing a useless vaccine that may have been responsible for its inventor, Noguchi Hideyo's, death when he believed he had immunity, as well as questionable ethical testing practices. This led to the Rockefeller Foundation quietly closing the program down (McGoey 2015, p.150). The mixed results for yellow fever vaccines, and the fact that it has not been eradicated 100 years later, suggest that it is a disease that may be better managed through public health programmes.

The Foundation in those early years also chose as a matter of principle to work with government agencies, rather than NGOs, as it felt it could gain more policy traction with governments, and influence the direction of their work (Farley 2004; Akami 2017). The idea was to promote technical approaches, with which US institutions could be involved, under the condition that '... the IHB lend a hand only on the invitation of an official agency' (Rockefeller Foundation 1925, p.11). The major exception to this, and in some ways curious, was the work in China which will be looked at in more detail below.

The 1920s, following the Versailles Peace Conference of 1919 and the new post-World War I dispensation, created opportunities for the Foundation and its health programme (Youde 2013; Smith 2009). One of the first acts of the newly created League of Nations (LoN) at its inaugural meeting in 1920, was to set up an international health organisation, which came into being in 1922, as the League of Nations Health Organization (LNHO) and in 1946, morphed into the UN's World Health Organization (WHO). The LNHO came just at the same time the Foundation and its nascent IHD were spreading their wings internationally, and LNHO provided a vehicle for the Foundation's work, while the IHC provided a model on which to base the LNHO, and later the WHO (Youde 2013, p.144).

The Foundation was also very useful for the US political elites given the Congressional veto of the US joining the League, despite President Woodrow Wilson's instrumental role in its establishment. In lieu of the US being directly part of the League, the Foundation was able to help fill the gaps and provide a conduit for US voices in the League.

[The Foundation's] aim was to create a global government of experts capable of solving the problems posed by the First World War and the crisis of 1929. While this diplomacy was presented as being wholly apolitical, it nevertheless had a clear objective that it held in common with American internationalist circles: to involve the United States in the LoN system to the maximum degree possible.

(Tournès 2014, p.323)

More specifically, the Foundation came to be seen as a saviour for the LNHO, as almost immediately it was under severe budget constraints with League members unwilling to fund what they saw as a very large budget to undertake the workplan. The LNHO allayed their fears by asking the Foundation through the IHD whether it could provide significant support outside the LoN funding cap. While this support was less than 5 per cent of the Foundation's overall budget after an initial start-up grant of $344,000 (~$30 million GDP adjusted) it was around half of the LNHO's core budget until the League was wound up in the late 1930s. Most of the global health funding came from the IHD, much of which went to LNHO field offices and their local priorities (Rockefeller Foundation 1922, 1932). This arrangement was not without its tensions with arguments in the IHD through the 1930s that they should limit their LNHO funding, and focus on their own international health work (Youde 2013; Weindling 1997, p.144).

The trade-off was that the IHD had very big say in the LNHOs programme, particularly at a central level, and the focus of the IHD on disease control and the: 'elimination of communicable disease' (Weindling 1997, p.145). In contrast to the hookworm eradication public health programme the IHD had undertaken a decade earlier, the IHD prioritised vector control, drug development, and vaccine research, while the not insubstantial public health programme was conducted at a local level largely off the radar of the IHD central office (Akami 2016, 2017). For the next 100 years this was to be a feature of the Foundation: that is, the belief on technological fixes to what are often, in part at least, social problems; a practice that was to be repeated by the Gates' Foundation nearly 100 years later.

In the case of public health, it often set field officers against laboratory personnel: 'They would have no truck with barefoot doctors or the Soviet Feldshers doctors assistants or engaging in public health issues' and the training tended to be based in the 'civilised climes of Toronto and London' (Farley 2004, p.6).

While IHD concentrated on its research, LNHO funds focused on training public health officers in modern public health practices and infusing proper hygiene training procedures. In this way, both LNHO and IHD could concentrate on their areas of expertise … By emphasising the importance of a biomedical perspective on public health and elevating it above social considerations, IHD ensured that scientific research and drug development played a significant role in international public health.

(Youde 2013, p.146)

At a central level the IHD support of the LNHO was mainly given to the technical solutions while public health was seen as secondary. The IHD argued that public health was dependent on state systems but '…politicians and diplomats representing nation states were often indifferent if not openly hostile to public health questions' (Weindling 1997, p.280). In the field, however, the IHD head office had little control over what happened, and the public health programmes became an inevitable, and largely hidden, part of the picture. The Foundation funded much of the Eastern Bureau of the LNHO, and much of this went to public health 'rural hygiene and rural recon-struction', such as the IHD public health education programme in East Java (Akami 2017, p.16), and establishing public health schools in Calcutta (now Kolkata), and Manila (Rockefeller Foundation 2020a).

Across Asia, public health programmes supported by the IHD flourished, largely because of excellent regional offices being able to act autonomously, such as pushing for public health reform in Siam (now Thailand). The IHD's work in East Asia on public health and rural reconstruction sought out local voices to be heard in much of the work that was done, as well as in the various LNHO offices at the time (Akami 2017). This is another example of the technocratic vision of the Foundation being subverted by local reality, and IHD leaders on the ground who were very competent, independent, and under-stood that reality (Akami 2016). The same pattern can be seen in agricultural research with the Green Revolution discussed later in the chapter, and as is evident in the China case, these simplistic binary arguments around technology hid a much more complex reality.

China

The focus on working with government research institutes as 'short term to stimulate self-help' was central to the IHD's approach across Asia and elsewhere (Farley 2004, p.4). China was a curious exception to the focus on working through governments, where the US missionary societies instead of the Chinese government were a central part. This had its origins in the active interest that John D. Rockefeller and his son had in China, and through Reverend Gates, the various missionary societies in China in the late 19th century. The Boxer rebellion of 1899–1901 against Western and Christian interests, and the West's (including the US) military response may explain Rockefeller's focus away from the Chinese government, as elements of the Chinese government including the Imperial Army of China supported the Boxer rebellion by a nationalist martial arts militia the *Yihequan*, which was loosely translated as Boxers (Ninkovich 1984; Esherick 1987).

There was also an element of the Anglophile, and an almost racist distrust of the Chinese in favour of Westerners, including western missionaries. The aim was to 'channel China's modernization in a liberal direction' and this was to continue for over 40 years (Ninkovich 1984, p.799). This project was largely unsuccessful as China was riven with conflict for most on the inter-war period. The Chinese Nationalist government founded by Sun Yat Sen in 1912 suffered a long period of instability following his death in 1925: there was an ongoing civil war between the Nationalist government of Chiang Kai-shek and the communist party led by Mao Zedong, as well as the Japanese invasion of Manchuria in 1931 and the subsequent war. The combined conflict lasted until 1949 and the establishment of the Communist government.

In 1909, prior to the establishment of the Foundation but certainly in anticipation of it, a six volume report was prepared for John D. Rockefeller II on how the nascent Foundation could work in China. The key element of this work was to set up an elite research hospital and medical centre, the Peking Union Medical College (PUMC), governed by an increasingly autonomous China Medical Board (Fosdick 1952). The original plan was to set up a University modelled on the University of Chicago, but the idea of a secular education was anathema to the missionary societies, and so in 1914 the Foundation settled on supporting a medical centre (Ninkovich 1984). The centre, with 59 buildings, was opened in 1919 with 25 per cent Chinese staff; by 1927 it had two-thirds Chinese staff; and by 1947 was fully staffed by Chinese nationals. In 1928 the China Medical Board broke away from the Foundation and was constituted as an independent agency to distribute the Foundation funds. For the next 20 years it was to run as a medical centre largely independent of both the Chinese government and the Foundation. The Foundation's aim for this broad project was to move China along to a more liberal society by way of example.

While it did important work in health, the move to a liberal society did not happen, in part due to the dysfunction of the Chinese government, which led to frustration within the Foundation (Ninkovich 1984). At the same time the IHD had moved from the public health work in disease management in the early 1920s 'to prioritizing the [IHD's] role in cutting-edge laboratory medical research' in the late 1920s and 1930s through the medical centre (Akami 2016, p.14).

The paradox was that the East Asia regional office of the IHD through the LNHO, however, was working with the Chinese nationalist government to reform the public health administration with the belief that 'the Chinese experts, not foreign advisers, had to take charge of their own national reforms' (Akami 2017, p.20). The Rockefeller IHD also worked through PUMC on public health, despite its elite medical research focus (Akami 2016). For example, the IHD East Asia Bureau, from 1930 to 1939, supported a programme that saw 5.6 million people immunised against plague in Shanghai.

In China, the Foundation's legacy was to be long lasting as the IHD work in the 1930s set in train a public health programme and the well-known Chinese barefoot doctors; the PUMC became the Chinese Academy of Medical Sciences with the Capital Hospital as part of it. Many of the graduates from the 1930s programmes carried on the important work, continuing to follow the Foundation's aims of eradicating disease, as part of the Chinese revolutionary government (Bullock 1980).

Economic

The other major work the Foundation undertook during the inter-war years was in developing a global team of technocrats to solve some of the inter-war economic problems. This resulted in support for a number of institutions globally, and while they were not directly looking at international development, they were a key part of what was to become the post-World War II global development architecture, which would be used in the Global South, and by networks built up by the Foundation, through its earlier work with both refugees and the economic department. The Foundation helped these University departments move from Europe to the US at the outbreak of war (Tournès 2014; Rockefeller Foundation 1939; Gary 1996).

The Foundation also helped institutions such as the London School of Economics and Political Science (LSE), and for possibly ideological reasons, ignored Cambridge and the leading economists there including John Maynard Keynes and Joan Robinson, probably because of their strong theoretical approach, and for supporting state intervention (Craver 1986). The Foundation's aim was to preserve 'the social order of capitalist democracy' in the face of more socialist pressures from the Great Depression, that both Keynes and Robinson represented (Abir-Am 1982, p.343).

The UK links the Foundation built were important as they had a large influence on the post-World War II economic development scene. Generally, at the time, the Foundation did not favour the social sciences, but exceptions were made, such as economics, anthropology, and international relations. Certain approaches, such as empirical economics and functional anthropology in particular, were in line with the colonial project of the subjugation of local populations and the preservation of a 'white' leadership (p.343). Part of this was eugenics research, a more controversial aspect of the Foundation work in the inter-war period, not only in the US but also elsewhere (Gunn 1999). In Nazi Germany with the Rockefeller Foundation support, the Kaiser Wilhelm Institute of Anthropology, Human Heredity, and Eugenics (KWIA) as well as others were funded (Black 2003). The racist and anti-Semitic attitudes of many of the liberal elite were seldom far from the surface, and some of the anthropology work of the time fed these myths (Gould 1996). This is a part of the Rockefeller Foundation history that tends to be overlooked in official accounts.

By the late 1930s support for these social sciences had fallen out of favour:

> He [Raymond Fosdick the President of the Foundation] thought the social sciences lacked the 'concreteness' of the medical and natural sciences. Whereas the support given to research on yellow fever had led to tangible results that promised to benefit humanity, the millions spent in support of basic research in the social sciences had not given similar results.
>
> (Craver 1986, p.217)

World War II did help revive some of the Foundation's work in economics when the Foundation was instrumental in helping Jewish scholars among others flee Europe in response to Nazi oppression through the 1930s. Over half of the more than 300 were social scientists who were placed in various institutions, and from 1940 their salaries were covered for the first few years. Most of these refugees went on to have permanent positions (Craver 1986; Gary 1996; Rockefeller Foundation 1939, 1940). The irony of funding the eugenics research used to justify the holocaust, and the rescue of Jewish scholars did not seem to bother the Foundation in any accounts of the time, but likewise, it still has not been acknowledged. While the population work of the 1950s under John D. Rockefeller III may have emerged from the vestiges of eugenics, the Foundation quickly moved away from this legacy.

The Foundation also helped in the move of the LoN's and others European research institutes. In 1940 the LoN's Economic, Financial, and Transit Department (EFTD) moved from Geneva to Princeton University in the United States, and with Foundation support it was able to continue all of its work during World War II to: '… make a major intellectual contribution to the reorganisation of the global economic order after 1945' (Tournès 2014, p.324). The academic rescue work was to be a forerunner of the refugee work the Foundation undertook post-war, and its role in the World Health Organization (Youde 2013). In 1943 the first major intergovernmental agency, the United Nations Relief and Rehabilitation Agency (UNRRA), saw the transition from the League to the UN and ultimately to the WHO. It had major Rockefeller Foundation involvement, not only in terms of staff, but also directions and ways of operating modelled on the IHD (Tournès 2014).

> It was thanks to this logic that it contributed to importing European expertise in the field of global economics into the United States. As such, it contributed as much as or even more than European actors towards carrying forward the legacy of the LoN within the United Nations.
>
> (Tournès 2014, p.399)

This was how the Foundation effortlessly moved from its role in LoN's health programmes to an even greater role in the nascent UN and the WHO in particular, at least in their formative years. The role of the Foundation in the health field has declined since the establishment of the WHO, but the WHO had inherited a strong legacy of from the Rockefeller Foundation, which has persisted, and even enhanced with its engagement of the Gates Foundation in the 21st century (Birn and Richter 2017). By the 2000s the Rockefeller Foundation support had shifted to population-based healthcare and family planning, but the health programme continues to be the largest of the Foundations areas with $15.3 billion being allocated between 1994 and 2011 (Youde 2013, p.148).

Agriculture

The agriculture work of the Rockefeller Foundation is most associated with the Green Revolution and the Nobel Peace prize winning work of Norman Borlaug, and his Foundation colleagues. It had its origins, however, more than half a century earlier when John D. Rockefeller through the General Education Board (GEB) in 1906 became involved in the Boll Weevil campaign in the US, with what the Rockefellers called 'scientific agriculture' (Fitzgerald 1986; Smith 2009a). It was based on an 'idealized yeomanry', a Jeffersonian ideal for a stable political economy based on smallholder farmers, as an attempt to address the marginalisation of white farmers on unviable land (Mitchell and Lowe 1990, p.324). This early work led to the establishment of the US extension service and the idea of farmer demonstrations in new technologies (Smith 2009a). It also laid the basis for the general philosophy of the Foundation, which it has generally followed over time:

> ... above all, to be done right 'the thing ought to be done by experts'. This was a lesson that transcended farming and even the need to settle the agrarian question. It was also a lesson that lay at the heart to the progressive consensus.
>
> (Mitchell and Lowe 1990, p.331)

The work of the GEB board in the South started with a $1 million grant by John D. Rockefeller in 1902, which was to grow to $2 million dollars by 1914. This work with white farmers was aimed at challenging both the populist and more left-leaning social movements at the time. The belief of the GEB was '... the contentment of the white agrarian class was key to southern economic and political stability' (Mitchell and Lowe 1990, p.325). Its aim was to focus on individual farms with demonstration plots with the latest technology and techniques to improve yields. It went beyond farmers, however, and also included a school programme, and programmes aimed at women such as tomato canning. At one point the canning programme had 30,000 clubs of women canning the tomatoes they grew on small plots (p.328).

This programme reached its peak from 1916 to 1920 when, in a radical move, it took over the Pearl River County and reformed education, agriculture, and other support services county-wide after which the County took back control in 1920. While it did not produce the major improvements in lives that was expected:

... the introduction of scientific agriculture played an important part in that stabilization by redirecting the 'uplift' of white yeomen away from the political solutions of the populists, socialists, and demagogues and toward the market solutions.

(Mitchell and Lowe 1990, p.330)

It was this work that led to its initial approaches for international agriculture development in the early years, re-emerging later in the 1930s, following feeding programmes with post-World War I refugees and other relief work (Fosdick 1952, p.28). This early agricultural research was originally tied in with the work of the International Institute of Agriculture founded in Rome in 1905 (Weindling 1997; Luzzatti 1906). This work intersected with the Foundation as it had a strong interest in nutrition, which the Foundation also had through emergency feeding programmes immediately after the war, which it desperately wanted to get out of as the Foundation had spent $22 million on these programmes. The last payment to the feeding programme was made in 1920 (Weindling 1997; Rockefeller Foundation 1918, p.271). However, the Foundation still continued to monitor nutrition programmes through the LNHO into the 1930s (p.277), and it continued to provide grants for agriculture through the International Education Board and others through the 1920s and 1930s (Rockefeller Foundation 1928, 1935, 1937).

A change by the Foundation's Trustees in 1933 to move from large-scale support to fewer recipients, to a strategy of funding many 'targets' on a smaller scale (Abir-Am 1982, p.348), led to the nascent agriculture research being absorbed into the microbiology programme, a flagship of the Foundation's new approach. The issue was that agriculture was not a real priority, except for some field programmes in China and exploratory work in Mexico (Rockefeller Foundation 1935; Fitzgerald 1986).

In the 1930s, the Foundation wanted a more empirical scientific approach to its work, and under Warren Weaver, the head of the powerful Division of Natural Sciences, the focus shifted away from farm demonstration work to more laboratory based work on molecular biology for improved plant breeding. This was to be part of the 'The Science of Man' [sic] newly established scientific agenda (Smith 2009a, p.464). Through the 1930s:

Molecular biology and scientific agriculture were concurrently and interactively shaped within and through the Foundation's sweeping agenda for the 'Science of Man' program.

(Smith 2009a, p.464)

For Weaver even including agriculture at that level, until the 1940s, was grudging at best (Weaver 1933, 1938), despite it being highlighted in the 1928 review (Rockefeller Foundation 1928). However, the agricultural work in the field, similar to public health, continued largely unabated. The work in China and also some tentative work in Mexico, was carried out on a smaller scale and like public health, flew under the head office radar.

For Weaver, however, a strong technocratic approach was key, where:

> ... people in the 'developing world' are each viewed as similar or even the same, therefore making intervention simpler through a set of generic and replicable programs and policies.
>
> (Smith 2009a, p.463)

This was, and continues to be, a common error in much scientific work, not least in international development. The shift away from agricultural production and nutrition reflected the same tensions as in health funding discussed above. But Warren Weaver wanted a clean break and focus on technical advances in health and agriculture through pure science well away from the users of these technical advances: '...the Division has wisely fostered a programme in pure science without reference to human welfare' (Weaver 1939, p.4). In agriculture, if it was to have focus, Weaver favoured using microbiology to address issues of disease on the one hand, and poor productivity on the other (Perkins 1990). This 'scientific' approach, however, was to be fairly short lived so that by the 1950s the exigencies of the Cold War and post-war development called for more applied locally based approaches.

In practice, the focus on evidence based laboratory science was more complex, and similar to health and economics, required field trials, so that by the 1940s agriculture research shifted back to be more applied, with Weaver being led along by the exigencies of war.

> ... but during the past year or two the officers have gradually moved towards an opportunistic attitude of funding programs [as] ... at the present moment practical aspects naturally a priority, receive special consideration.
>
> (Weaver 1942a, p.1)

By the 1940s field trials were taking place in Mexico under the Foundation's Mexico Agricultural Program. This marked a shift back to the applied agricultural approaches of the turn of the century in the southern US, with a reluctant Warren Weaver being brought on board

(Smith 2009a; Kilby 2019; Fitzgerald 1986). This change of heart was mainly due the need to assist the Mexican government at a time when it was an important friend to the US, but also the advantage agricultural science might give the US later in the Cold War struggle with the Soviet Union (Perkins 1990, p.11).

Agricultural science funding rose from 1 per cent of expenditure in 1939–1943, to 15 per cent in 1944, due to not only increases *per se,* but to war-imposed cuts in other areas (Rockefeller Foundation 1945). By 1951 the Science Division was renamed the Division of Natural Sciences and Agriculture, which in some ways represented a comedown for the purist Weaver, who was to remain head of the Division for a few more years (Rockefeller Foundation 1949). The other key element of the technocratic approach was that the science was intended to be 'value neutral to scale', the implication being a natural bias to larger production units given economies of scale (Fitzgerald 1986, p.458).

This shift away from pure science occurred when John D. Rockefeller III (grandson of the founder) was the Chair and large scale changes within the Foundation occurred. The remit of the Foundation broadened away from support for pure science in US universities, to have a stronger focus in the Global South. Rockefeller's motives were very much driven by the Cold War, which also a had the attention of the Ford Foundation: 'Sovereignty gaps, looming food deficits and unrestrained population growth were considered the "perfect storm" for communist subversion' (Nally and Taylor 2015, p.15). Rockefeller III was also a huge supporter of the arts, and he drove some the subtle shifts in development funding to institutional support of Southern Institutions in the 1960s. In agriculture research there was also a shift under Rockefeller III to look at the farming systems, and not just the technology of production:

> [these] ideas were quickly absorbed by the Rockefeller Foundation, and diffused internationally, not simply because they reflected fashionable thinking in behavioural economics, but because they seemed to align in a rather seamless and natural way with the philanthropic goal of 'self-help' practiced more than half a century earlier by Seaman Knapp of the General Education Board [a precursor of the Foundation].
>
> (Nally and Taylor 2015, p.20)

Rockefeller would have been well aware of Knapp's work with the GEB, as their work with smallholder farmers in the US South would have been part of his childhood.

The Green Revolution

The Green Revolution was to be the flagship programme of the Foundation post-World War II, following some earlier work in the 1930s. The Foundation had been involved in plant breeding research at Nanking University that was expanded and used in rural reconstruction in 1935, which it then had to abandon with the onset of war and the Japanese invasion (Fosdick 1952, p.184). But it was Nelson Rockefeller's direct involvement in Mexico following nascent attempts in 1933 when the Foundation's director for health and the US ambassador had some preliminary discussions. These came to nothing, especially after the Mexican government seized US assets including Rockefeller's own Standard Oil in 1938 (Perkins 1990).

The opportunity for reconciliation came when the US-friendly President Camacho came to power in 1940, and US vice-president Henry A. Wallace undertook a symbolic road to trip the Mexico to attend the inauguration. Wallace's trip to Mexico and his observations on the state of agriculture laid the groundwork for the Foundation to be involved, and Fosdick, the head of the Foundation, sent a survey team to Mexico in 1941. This gave it the necessary prestige to ensure that it would be accepted by the Mexican government, and would be less likely to fail or be marginalised. The aim was for Mexico to achieve food security and reduce the risk of an anti-US and possible communist government taking over. It was also timely as the Foundation had to withdraw from Europe due to the war, and it was looking for new areas of investment. The political exigencies both within the US government and Foundation itself saw a move back into operational programmes in Mexico, but over the following 20 years this operational approach would be replicated India, and elsewhere as well.

The upshot of Fosdick's Mexico survey was the establishment of a semi-autonomous Office of Special Studies, to advise the Mexican government. Its first task was to establish the Mexico Agricultural Program and an associated research station, to be staffed by the top plant breeders of the time. It still echoed some of the Foundations work of the 1930s onwards and was a highly technical scientific approach to agricultural research. However, there were farmer demonstrations pushed for by Norman Borlaug (Kilby 2019), possibly a deliberate nod back to the GEB work in the South of the US at the turn of the century, where farmer demonstrations were a central feature.

The long term result of this initial work in the 1940s was the very successful adoption in Mexico and India of improved varieties, mainly of wheat, in the 1960s and 1970s, which collectively became known as the Green Revolution. This was a term coined by USAID Administrator William Gaud in 1968, in part to contrast itself with the Red Revolution of the Soviet Union and China. Norman Borlaug, however, would without any sense of irony in the early 2000s name China as the success story of the Green Revolution. China had a parallel programme that emulated some of the techniques of the Foundation without engaging with it, but it had a much larger social component, and therefore a greater reach and success, at least until the 1990s (Kilby 2019).

The Green Revolution in Mexico and India was only successful for those crops for which a known supply of inputs including water and fertiliser could be assured. In Mexico that was wheat grown by the larger farms in the north of the country which had access to irrigation. In the centre and south of the country where maize was grown by poorer and indigenous farmers the success rate was much lower as they tended to hedge their bets and plant high yielding varieties in rainfed areas as a smaller proportion of the total crop, with other varieties selected for drought or wind tolerance.

The other aspect of the Green Revolution is the role of national government in policy settings. Both in Mexico and India, for different political reasons, larger farmers were targeted in the programme as in both cases it was a case of increasing national production and weaning the respective countries off imports from the US. The unstated reason was to avoid any US dependency and the associated political pressure it could have for national decision making, which is what occurred in the mid-1960s in India (Kilby 2019). In Mexico it was case of providing food to support '... development based on "private enterprise" and modernization after the capitalist model' (Brinkmann 2009, p.5). Increasing national production took precedence over equity considerations.

As Bell noted in relation to the Ford Foundation '[Ford Foundation] ... centre managers give more weight to equity issues than national government officials' (Bell 1981, p.6). This would be similar to the Rockefeller Foundation, at least for their East Asia office (e.g. see Akami 2017). One of the enduring myths of the Green Revolution is that the unequal outcomes were a result of the research itself rather than conscious national government policy. Critiques of the Green Revolution that it led to widening inequality and favouring wealthier farmers are valid, but the trade-off between national level food security and local equity issues were very real, a trade-off that national governments grappled with at the time.

The key consideration was the role of the research in focusing on these the technologies, the role of local policy makers who were faced with what they saw as an existential crisis, and how technology could be developed in the full understanding of the social implications. The Rockefeller Foundation understood this in the early 1960s:

> [an earlier] assumption that American know how and improved materials could rather easily be transferred to foreign environments and that vigorous extension campaigns were about all that was needed to carry the good word to a benighted peasantry ... [now] conditions of the local environment, social as well as biological were a requisite first step to the improvement of agricultural production.
>
> (Rockefeller Foundation 1962, pp.2–3)

The Foundation spread its wings further in agriculture research in 1953 when John D. Rockefeller III set up The Agricultural Development Council (ADC) following a survey trip to the Far East (Cleaver 1972; Nally and Taylor 2015). The Rockefeller Foundation then joined with the Ford Foundation in 1960 to set up International Rice Research Institute (IRRI) in the Philippines to develop improved varieties of rice. A little later CYMMIT was established in Mexico in 1965, taking over the existing agricultural wheat research programme of the Mexican government. What set IRRI and CYMMIT apart is that they were much less centred on US researchers and were much more multinational in their focus. These were important initiatives and it is worth noting that by 2005, 60 per cent of the world's rice was planted with IRRI bred varieties.

What was clear by the 1960s was that as the issue of improved production was solved then the wider problems of agricultural and the local social systems became more evident (Rockefeller Foundation 1961, p.22). Increasing urban development and the migration to cities continues to see agricultural research focus on large-scale production systems to provide a voracious urban population who not only seek more, but higher value, food. The issue was that the small scale peasant farmer invariably missed out.

India

The story of the Rockefeller Foundation in India, one of its notable success stories, is one of longer term relationships, and to some extent a distancing from the US government, particularly in the 1960s. The Rockefeller Foundation came to India in the 1950s not long after independence in 1947. Warren Weaver had earlier identified India (with China) as focal point for its agricultural work as early as 1946 (Weaver 1946). The Indian government under Nehru was undertaking a nation-building programme at the political, social, and economic level, but with at the same time with a struggling rural sector and fragile food security. It was also a period of Cold War rivalry with both the US and Soviet Union courting India, while Nehru had a vision of India being at the head of a nascent non-aligned movement.

The Foundation work in India followed the Mexico work and used much of that research to jump-start high-yielding cereal production (mainly wheat) in India from the 1950s and into the late 1960s and early 1970s. While Foundations staff made their first foray into India in the late 1920s early 1930s with public health and hygiene (Rockefeller Foundation 1929), in the 1950s it moved to agriculture, when they provided technical training to the Indian agricultural research institutes from 1953 to 1974 (Lele and Goldsmith 1989, p.309). There was little research capacity in India at independence apart from the Imperial Agricultural Research Institute that sponsored some work on wheat breeding prior to independence (Perkins 1990).

The Foundation training was:

> … extremely modest $7.9m million, over the entire period and never involved more than a dozen expatriates at a time. It is one of the outstanding examples of catalytic aid where a donor stimulates improvements in recipient institutions that enable them to develop an indigenous capacity to adapt more productive technology.
>
> (Lele and Goldsmith 1989, p.309)

This work was somewhat different to the approach taken by the Rockefeller Foundation in Mexico where the Foundation led with their own ideas. The India programme was, in concert with USAID, based on support to agricultural universities, and so deploying and organising existing agricultural research in India. At the same time the Ford Foundation, with land grant universities, was supporting agricultural education and extension, as well as a very large community development programme through the 1950s. As Subramaniam (1968) noted a few years later, this was critical to the later success. For the Rockefeller Foundation this represented a marked shift from the 1930s and its highly technical approach.

The initial Rockefeller Foundation work in India was less successful, focussing on maize, at the suggestion of Indian officials (Perkins 1990; Lele and Goldsmith 1989) and bringing in the varieties from Mexico.

But this programme proved the model could work, and it moved to wheat, and to a lesser extent rice (Rockefeller Foundation 1964b). The key elements of the India programme were to cooperate with existing institutions rather than build new ones as had been the case in Latin America; a long time-horizon of ten years or more, and thus distinguishing themselves from shorter term bilateral programs; and finally, the Foundations provided the marginal input needed to raise to very high standards what the national government was already doing. To do this the Foundation '... was determined that its senior staff on India should be individuals whose credentials would ensure that their advice carried weight with their Indian counterparts' (Lele and Goldsmith 1989, p.316). As noted above, issues of equity and distribution were not a priority for the Indian government, which was in the middle of a national food crisis that was being used by the US government to gain leverage and shift India from being non-aligned in the Cold War to the US camp. But as Perkins notes, Warren Weaver and George Harrar and senior Foundation staff were probably not at all interested in equity anyway:

> It is doubtful that Weaver and Harrar thought deeply about the caste/class structure of India and its relation to agriculture, food, and hunger. They assumed caste and superstition were barriers to improved productivity, but they did not follow their thoughts with an analysis of distribution.
>
> (Perkins 1990, p.14)

The problems in India were also a little different. Under colonial rule agriculture had stagnated (Gupta 2019), and even after independence the large scale investment in irrigation and a ten-fold increase in fertiliser use over the same time pushed the cumulative cereal grains growth to only 3 per cent from 1950 to 1965, barely enough to keep up with the burgeoning population, and so left India very vulnerable. As Subramaniam, the minister at the time, noted the new varieties were simply not available in India, and so dwarf varieties that did not fall over (lodge) under irrigation and greater fertiliser use, had to be brought in (Subramaniam 1968). The new varieties from Mexico resulted in almost immediate results, and set India onto a growth path in agriculture, providing the food security for growth in other areas, the most important being the service sector. 'Public investment in agriculture tripled between 1960 and 1980 [and] yield per acre doubled in rice production by 1990, and tripled in wheat production' (Gupta 2019, p.820).

The Rockefeller Foundation was perfectly placed to fill the gap in the development plans for India at the time. While the US government under President Johnson was pressuring the Indian government to open up its economy to allow US investment and shift away from its socialist tendencies, the agricultural successes enabled India to have the space to chart its own direction. It was able to use the Green Revolution to move politically to the 'left' with its social policies, including nationalising the banks, while also lifting restrictions on foreign investment in industry (Kilby 2019). While this may not have been what the Foundation intended, it did provide the basis for a more independent and non-aligned approach in India's development and position in the world.

By the 1960s the focus of the Foundation in India also moved to institutional support, and this mirrored that of the land grant universities in the US. Innovations in post graduate teaching of the Indian Agricultural Research Institutes were being adopted by state universities (Rockefeller Foundation 1964b, p.6), supported by a large focus on fellowships and scholarships locally and to the US (Rockefeller Foundation 1964a).

The Rockefeller Foundation post 1970s

After the success of the Green Revolution in the 1960s into the 1970s and the decline of the pure science of Warren Weaver, the Foundation had reached a crossroads. The 1960s and 1970s were turbulent times for all Foundations not least Rockefeller, with falling income due to the falling value of the endowment as a result of the 1970s economic turmoil. From the 1950s the work shifted from support of European research institutions to focus more clearly on developing countries

> ... under Dean Rusk (1952–61) the RF began to withdraw support from Europe and shifted it to the newly emerging nations. Still maintained its academic character with divisions structured along academic lines with each being fairly autonomous. Harrar moved it from the library and laboratory into the fields and streets.
>
> (Rockefeller Foundation 1971, p.5)

The shift to a clearer development focus also moved from the technical, to include the social in the '... the development of their cultural resources' and long-term development of their research capacity through institutional grants (Rockefeller Foundation 1961, p.14). In 1964 the focus of the work was broadened to: '1 the conquest of hunger; 2 the population problem; 3 strengthening emerging centres of learning; 4 equal opportunity; 5 cultural development' (Rockefeller Foundation 1964b, p.1).

The latter two priorities under John D. Rockefeller III were quite a shift from the technocrat years and started to resemble the focus of the Ford Foundation, and respond to the social shifts in the US, including the civil rights movement, but also cultural shifts with a massive grant to the develop the New York Lincoln Center, of which John D. Rockefeller III was also chair (1952–1972) (Rockefeller Foundation 1963). The work in international development in supporting emerging centres of learning was built on some of the earlier work in India so that by 1966 seven universities in the Global South were receiving long-term development support to strengthen their teaching and research (Rockefeller Foundation 1966, p.52). The 'conquest of hunger' was also to be a focus at least until the 1980s when it was wound back with the comment in the 1981 annual report that it was 'a title that may fall under the ban on hubris' (Rockefeller Foundation 1981, p.21).

The 1970s were to be a watershed for all Foundations, driven by a change in the regulatory environment that narrowed the flexibility Foundations had in what they funded and how much. A key requirement was that they were required to spend at least 5 per cent of their endowment, or all of the income, whichever was greater, on Foundation purposes. This had the effect of distorting investment strategies and encouraging a higher growth high-risk approach. This proved catastrophic in the high inflation stagnant growth, low dividend environment of the 1970s. The Rockefeller Foundation, in retrospect, would have preferred a simple rule of at least 5 per cent of the endowment being disbursed (Rockefeller Foundation 1980).

Following the death of John D. Rockefeller III in 1978, and the turbulent decade of the 1970s, there was a major rethink with a shift back to the more technocratic approach of the pre-war years. By 1981 the education for development programme was being phased out after 20 years, field staff fell from 136 in the 1960s to 34 in 1981, and there was a move back to more pure science. There was an accompanying shift away from the hubris of the 'conquest of hunger', and the population programs were all put under the microscope (Rockefeller Foundation 1981). By the 1983 a new programme direction with an 'expansion of RF support for basic biological research' including genetic engineering and molecular biology, and all agricultural field staff were 'withdrawn in an orderly fashion'(Rockefeller Foundation 1983, pp.xv,1). The ghost of Warren Weaver had re-appeared.

A decade later the cycle continued with another shift away from science and back to:

> ... nine core strategies: mobilisation for unmet demand ($14.2m); crop yield, by 2015, 50% increase in maize productivity; population based healthcare; female education; school reform; leadership in environment and development; community building; understanding and negotiating difference across changing societies; energy transition.
>
> (Rockefeller Foundation 1993, p.11)

The key difference in the 1990s was the shift to the more managerial approaches of the time, with management setting targets for programmes to achieve, come what may. By the 21st century, the Foundation had its endowment base fall in part due to the economic downturn and lower returns, particularly in the 1970s, and also partly due to deliberate decisions at various times to wind it down.

While the technical focus remained there had been a much greater focus in penetrating existing systems with market-based neoliberal ideas to expand health and agriculture business opportunities at the expense of government (Smith 2009b). In 2006 with the Gates Foundation, the Rockefeller Foundation set up the Alliance for Green Revolution in Africa (AGRA), a granting agency for African research institutes with a strong focus on technical research and commercial inputs that lie largely out of reach of the peasant farmer (Ejeta 2010; Shilomboleni 2017; Toenniessen, Adesina, and DeVries 2008). However, by the 2010s the Rockefeller Foundation policy influence had waned and become eclipsed by the Gates' Foundation. Much of the Foundation's work, while important, began to resemble that of any number of large NGOs, and its role in public policy and advocacy in international development had truly diminished.

Conclusion

The Rockefeller Foundation was the first of the great foundations involved in international development. It moved into the global sphere as soon as it could at the end of World War I with a focus initially on health for 20 years up until World War II, and then of agriculture for the 20 years after the war. It struggled with an almost ideological belief in the pure sciences and what they could do, while at the same time a very effective field programme in public health and agricultural production provided the results it is most remembered for.

It also had an ambiguous and at times worrying relationship with the social sciences and humanities. Before World War II support for eugenics programs and vocational education for African Americans reflected a strongly racist view that prevailed among some elites, while at the same time supporting think-tanks and social and political science programmes in Europe and elsewhere between the wars so it had a voice in what the post-war world in the West would look like. When John D. Rockefeller III joined the board in the 1950s there was a clearer shift to the humanities and support for civil rights, and in the 1980s women's rights, gender issues, and anti-poverty programmes. Again there was a shift back to the pure sciences for a period after Rockefeller's death, but by the 2010s the Rockefeller Foundation seemed to have settled on liberal causes, but with much less focus on public policy. During the COVID-19 response the focus has been largely on the domestic US focusing on public health relief programmes and COVID testing, with $50 million to be provided over two years (Rockefeller Foundation 2020b). Much less, if any, additional funding has been targeted to the international program and COVID related public health in the Global South.

Note

1 The RCS closed after five years with its work absorbed into first the International Health Commission (IHC) of the Foundation in 1913, then the International Health Board (IHB) from 1916.

References

Abir-Am, Pnina. 1982. 'The Discourse of Physical Power and Biological Knowledge in the 1930s: A Reappraisal of the Rockefeller Foundation's Policy in Molecular Biology.' *Social Studies of Science* 12 (3):341–382.

Akami, Tomoko. 2016. 'Victor Heiser and the Rockefeller Foundation as a Medium for the Intercolonial Transfer of Health Management Knowledge in Asia in the Era of the League of Nations', in *Rockefeller Archive Center Research Reports*. Sleepy Hollow New York: Rockefeller Archive Center

Akami, Tomoko. 2017. 'Imperial polities, intercolonialism, and the shaping of global governing norms: public health expert networks in Asia and the League of Nations Health Organization, 1908–37'. *Journal of Global History* (1): 4–25.

Bell, David 1981. Memo to Thomas Franklin 'Report on International research centres, August 25', in Office of the Vice-President Frances Sutton Series II, edited by Rockefeller Archive Center: Ford Foundation Archives program files International Agricultural research Papers, Box 11, Folder 5.

Birn, Anne-Emanuelle, and Judith Richter. 2017. 'US Philanthrocapitalism and the global health agenda: the Rockefeller and Gates foundations, past and present', in *Health Care under the Knife: Moving Beyond Capitalism for our Health*, edited by Howard Waitzkin and the Working Group for Health Beyond Capitalism. New York: Monthly Review Press.

Black, Edwin. 2003. *War against the Weak: Eugenics and America's Campaign to Create a Master Race*. Washington: Dialog Press

Brinkmann, Mankel. 2009. 'Fighting world hunger on a global scale: The Rockefeller Foundation and the Green Revolution in Mexico.' Rockefeller Archive Center Research Reports Online [online]. http://www.rockarch.org/publications/resrep/brinkmann.pdf [Accessed 8 May 2012], edited by Rockefeller Foundation.

Bullock, Mary Brown. 1980. *An American Transplant: The Rockefeller Foundation and Peking Union Medical College*. Los Angeles: University of California Press.

Carnegie, Andrew. (1889)1906. 'The Gospel of Wealth'. *North American Review* 183 (599): 526–537.

Chernow, Ron. 1988. *Titan: The Life of John D. Rockefeller, Sr*. New York: Random House.

Cleaver, Harry M. 1972. 'The contradictions of the Green Revolution'. *The American Economic Review* 62 (1/2): 177–186.

Clarke, Gerard. 2019. 'The New Global Governors: Globalization, Civil Society, and the Rise of Private Philanthropic Foundations'. *Journal of Civil Society* 15 (3): 197–213.

Craver, Earlene. 1986. 'Patronage and the directions of research in economics: The Rockefeller Foundation in Europe, 1924–1938'. *Minerva* 24 (2): 205–222.

Ejeta, Gebisa. 2010. 'African Green Revolution needn't be a mirage'. *Science* 327 (5967): 831–832.

Ehrenreich, Barbara. 2010. *Nickel and Dimed: On (Not) Getting by in America*. New York: Metropolitan Books.

Esherick, Joseph W. 1987. *The Origins of the Boxer Uprising*. Berkeley: University of California Press.

Farley, John. 2004. *To cast out disease: a history of the International Health Division of Rockefeller Foundation (1913–1951)*. Oxford: Oxford University Press.

Fejerskov, Adam Moe. 2015. 'From Unconventional to Ordinary? The Bill and Melinda Gates Foundation and the Homogenizing Effects of International Development Cooperation'. *Journal of International Development* 27 (7): 1098–1112.

Fejerskov, Adam Moe. 2018. *The Gates Foundation's Rise to Power: Private Authority in Global Politics*. Abingdon: Routledge.

Fitzgerald, Deborah. 1986. 'Exporting American Agriculture: The Rockefeller Foundation in Mexico, 1943–53'. *Social Studies of Science* 16 (3): 457–483.

Fosdick, Raymond B. 1952. *The Story of the Rockefeller Foundation*. New York: Harper and Brothers.

Gary, Brett. 1996. 'Communication Research, the Rockefeller Foundation, and Mobilization for the War on Words, 1938–1944'. *Journal of Communication* 46 (3): 124–148.

Gates, Frederick. 1905a. Note to John D Rockefeller June 3. In Frederick Gates Collection, edited by Rockefeller Archive Center: Rockefeller Foundation Box 2 Accession no. 4 'The Financial Situation 1906'. The General Education Board 1903–1926 Folder 28.

Gates, Frederick. 1905b. Note to John D Rockefeller on World Philanthropy. In Frederick Gates Collection, edited by Rockefeller Archive Center: Rockefeller Foundation Box 2 Accession no. 4 'The Financial Situation 1906'. The General Education Board 1903–1926 Folder 28.

Gould, Stephen Jay. 1996. *The Mismeasure of Man*. New York: WW Norton & Company.

Gunn, Jennifer. 1999. 'A Few Good Men: The Rockefeller Approach to Population, 1911–1936, The Development of the Social Sciences in the United States and Canada: The Role of Philantrophy. 97–114.' In Theresa Richardson and Donald Fisher (eds) *The Development of the Social Sciences in the United States and Canada : The Role of Philanthropy*, 97–114. Stamford, CA: Ablex.

Gupta, Bishnupriya. 2019. 'Falling Behind and Catching up: India's Transition from a Colonial Economy'. *Economic History Review* 72 (3): 803–827.

Hinrichs, Albert Ford. 1923. *'The United Mine Workers of America and the Non-Union Coal Fields'*. *Business Fluctuations and the American Labor Movement,* issues 246–247. New York: Columbia University.

Jennings, Bruce H. 1988. *Foundations of international agricultural research: Science and politics in Mexican agriculture.* Boulder Co: Westview Press.

Kilby, Patrick. 2019. *The Green Revolution: narratives of politics, technology and gender.* Abingdon: Routledge.

Kohler, Robert E. 1976. 'The management of science: The experience of Warren Weaver and the Rockefeller Foundation programme in molecular biology'. *Minerva* 14 (3): 279–306.

Lele, Uma, and Arthur A.Goldsmith. 1989. 'The Development of National Agricultural Research Capacity: India's Experience with the Rockefeller Foundation and Its Significance for Africa'. *Economic Development and Cultural Change* 37 (2): 305–343.

Lippincott. 1913. 'The Unwilling Philanthropist'. *Lippincott's Monthly Magazine, a Popular Journal of General Literature,* 91, Philadelphia: J. B. Lippincott and Co.

Luzzatti, Luigi. 1906. 'The International Institute of Agriculture'. *The North American Review* 182 (594): 651.

McGoey, Linsey. 2015. *No Such Thing as a Free Gift: The Gates Foundation and the Price of Philanthropy.* London: Verso Books.

Mitchell, Theodore R., and Robert Lowe. 1990. 'To sow contentment: Philanthropy, scientific agriculture and the making of the new South: 1906–1920'. *Journal of Social History* 24 (2): 317–340.

Nally, David. 2015. 'The Politics of Self-Help: The Rockefeller Foundation, Philanthropy and the "Long" Green Revolution.' *Political Geography* 49: 51–63.

Nally, David, and Stephen Taylor. 2015. 'The politics of self-help: The Rockefeller Foundation, philanthropy and the 'long' Green Revolution'. *Political Geography* 49: 51–63.

Nielsen, Waldemar A. 1972. *The Big Foundations*. New York: Columbia University Press.

Ninkovich, Frank. 1984. 'The Rockefeller Foundation, China, and Cultural Change'. *The Journal of American History* 70 (4): 799–820.

Parmar, Inderjeet. 2012. *Foundations of the American Century: The Ford, Carnegie, and Rockefeller Foundations in the Rise of American Power*. New York: Columbia University Press.

Perkins, John H. 1990. 'The Rockefeller Foundation and the green revolution, 1941–1956'. *Agriculture and Human Values* 7 (3–4):6–18.

Rockefeller Foundation. 1914. 'Rockefeller Foundation annual report 1913–14'. Reading Room. Rockefeller Archive Center. Tarrytown NY.

Rockefeller Foundation. 1915. 'Rockefeller Foundation annual report 1915'. Reading Room. Rockefeller Archive Center. Tarrytown NY.

Rockefeller Foundation. 1916. 'Rockefeller Foundation annual report 1916'. Reading Room. Rockefeller Archive Center. Tarrytown NY.

Rockefeller Foundation. 1918. 'Rockefeller Foundation annual report 1918'. Reading Room. Rockefeller Archive Center. Tarrytown NY.

Rockefeller Foundation. 1921. 'Rockefeller Foundation annual report 1921'. Reading Room. Rockefeller Archive Center. Tarrytown NY.

Rockefeller Foundation. 1922. 'Rockefeller Foundation annual report 1922'. Reading Room. Rockefeller Archive Center, Tarrytown NY.

Rockefeller Foundation. 1925. 'Rockefeller Foundation annual report 1925'. Reading Room Rockefeller Archive Center, Tarrytown NY.

Rockefeller Foundation. 1928. 'Minutes and Office conferences 1927–1930 Natural sciences, May 23'. Rockefeller Archive. Administration, Program and Policy; Series 915 Program and Policy, Natural Sciences and Agriculture 1913–1934; Report Pro 10–16 1936–1938. Folder 1. Rockefeller Archive Center, Tarrytown NY.

Rockefeller Foundation. 1929. 'Rockefeller Foundation annual report 1929'. Reading Room. Rockefeller Archive Center, Tarrytown NY

Rockefeller Foundation. 1932. 'Rockefeller Foundation annual report 1932'. Reading Room. Rockefeller Archive Center, Tarrytown NY.

Rockefeller Foundation. 1935. 'Rockefeller Foundation annual report 1935'. Reading Room. Rockefeller Archive Center, Tarrytown NY.

Rockefeller Foundation. 1937. 'Rockefeller Foundation annual report 1937'. Reading Room. Rockefeller Archive Center, Tarrytown NY.

Rockefeller Foundation. 1939. 'Rockefeller Foundation annual report 1939'. Reading Room. Rockefeller Archive Center, Tarrytown NY.

Rockefeller Foundation. 1940. 'Rockefeller Foundation annual report 1940'. Reading Room. Rockefeller Archive Center, Tarrytown NY.

Rockefeller Foundation. 1945. Trustees Bulletin Dec issue. Administration, Program and Policy; Series 915 Program and Policy, Natural Sciences and Agriculture 1913–1934; Report Pro 10–16 1936–1938. Folder 4. Rockefeller Archive Center, Tarrytown NY.

Rockefeller Foundation. 1949. Excerpt from Minutes 6 April Natural Sciences. Administration, Program and Policy; Series 915 Program and Policy, Natural Sciences and Agriculture 1913–1934; Report Pro 10–16 1936–1938. Folder 4. Rockefeller Archive Center, Tarrytown NY.

Rockefeller Foundation. 1961. 'Rockefeller Foundation annual report 1961'. Reading Room. Rockefeller Archive Center, Tarrytown NY.

Rockefeller Foundation. 1962. Special meeting of the original board of Agricultural consultant to plan the 20th anniversary report on the Agricultural programs of the Rockefeller Foundation Aug 17, Box 4, 3.2 Administration, Program and Policy;Series 923 Program and Policy, Agriculture Folder 20. Rockefeller Archive Center. Tarrytown NY.

Rockefeller Foundation. 1963. Officers Conference March 5, List 203. Box 9, 3.2 Administration, Program and Policy; Series 904 Program and Policy, Officers Conferences 1959, Folder 63. Rockefeller Archive Center. Tarrytown NY.

Rockefeller Foundation. 1964a. Financial Summary Program in Agricultural Science 1941–1964. Box 4, 3.2 Administration, Program and Policy Series 923, Program and Policy, Agriculture Folder 16. Rockefeller Archive Center. Tarrytown NY

Rockefeller Foundation. 1964b. Meeting of the Board of consultants for Agricultural Science August 10–12, Tarrytown House. Box 4, 3.2 Administration, Program and Policy Series 923, Program and Policy, Agriculture Folder 15. Rockefeller Archive Center. Tarrytown NY.

Rockefeller Foundation. 1966. 'President's Review and Annual Report'. Reading Room. Rockefeller Archive Center. Tarrytown NY.

Rockefeller Foundation. 1971. 'President's Ten Year Review. Reading Room'. Rockefeller Archive Center. Tarrytown NY.

Rockefeller Foundation. 1980. 'Annual Report'. Reading Room. Rockefeller Archive Center. Tarrytown NY.

Rockefeller Foundation. 1981. 'Annual Report'. Reading Room. Rockefeller Archive Center. Tarrytown NY.

Rockefeller Foundation. 1983. Promoting international cooperation on critical food and Agricultural Issues (draft) Jan 14. Box 43, 3.2 Administration, Program and Policy Series 900 Program and Policy, Food Policy 1982–1984, 1986, Folder 226. Rockefeller Archive Center. Tarrytown NY.

Rockefeller Foundation. 1993. 'President's review and Annual Report'. Reading Room. Rockefeller Archive Center. Tarrytown NY.

Rockefeller Foundation. 2020a. 'Our History: A Closer Look Through The Years 1920'. *About Us*. https://www.rockefellerfoundation.org/about-us/our-history/. Accessed Aug 5. 2020.

Rockefeller Foundation. 2020b. 'Covid 19 Response'. https://www.rockefellerfoundation.org/covid-19-response/. Accessed Aug 14. 2020.

Shepherd, Chris J. 2005. 'Imperial science: The Rockefeller Foundation and Agricultural Science in Peru, 1940–1960'. *Science as Culture* 14 (2):113–137.

Shilomboleni, Helena. 2017. 'A sustainability assessment framework for the African green revolution and food sovereignty models in southern Africa'. *Cogent Food & Agriculture* 3 (1): 1–17.

Smith, Elta. 2009. 'Imaginaries of Development: The Rockefeller Foundation and Rice Research'. *Science as Culture* 18 (4): 461–482.

Subramaniam, C. 1968. 'India's Program for Agricultural Progress, Symposium Convened by the Rockefeller Foundation. Strategies for the conquest of Hunger', Symposium Convened by the Rockefeller Foundation, April 1 and 2, Rockefeller University. New York.

Tarbell, Ida Minerva. 1904. *The History of the Standard Oil Company.* New York: McClure, Phillips and Co.

Toenniessen, Gary, Akinwumi Adesina, and Joseph DeVries. 2008. 'Building an alliance for a green revolution in Africa'. *Annals of the New York Academy ofSsciences* 1136 (1): 233–242.

Tournès, Ludovic. 2014. 'The Rockefeller Foundation and the Transition from the League of Nations to the UN (1939–1946)'. *Journal of Modern European History* 12 (3): 323–341.

Trenton Evening Times. 1915. 'Congress to Curb Foundations'. *Trenton Evening Times*, August 26.

Weaver, Warren. 1933. Memo: the benefits from science Sciences and Foundation Program the proposed program January 27. Administration, Program and Policy; Series 915 Program and Policy, Natural Sciences and Agriculture 1913–1934; Report Pro 10–16 1936–1938. Folder 6. Rockefeller Archive Center. Tarrytown NY.

Weaver, Warren. 1938. Memo: October 17 'Basic research in natural sciences'. Administration, Program and Policy; Series 915 Program and Policy, Natural Sciences and Agriculture 1913–1934; Report Pro 10–16 1936–1938. Folder 3. Rockefeller Archive Center. Tarrytown NY.

Weaver, Warren. 1939. 'Report of the Committee of review, appraisal and advice. The RF Division of Natural scenes May'. Administration, Program and Policy; Series 915 Program and Policy, Natural Sciences and Agriculture 1938; Report Pro 17, Folder 12. Rockefeller Archive Center. Tarrytown NY.

Weaver, Warren. 1942a. 'Analysis of the Program in relation to changing world conditions', Preliminary divisional Statement used at Officers conference October 7. Administration, Program and Policy; Series 915 Program and Policy, Natural Sciences and Agriculture1938; Report Pro17, Folder 12. Rockefeller Archive Center. Tarrytown NY.

Weaver, Warren. 1942b. Warren Weaver memo to officers Oct 26. Administration, Program and Policy; Series 915 Program and Policy, Natural Sciences and Agriculture 1913–1934; Report Pro 10–16 1936–1938. Folder 4. Rockefeller Archive Center. Tarrytown NY

Weaver, Warren. 1946. Memo: Warren Weaver 26 September. Administration, Program and Policy; Series 915 Program and Policy, Natural Sciences and Agriculture 1913–1934; Report Pro 10–16 1936–1938. Folder 4. Rockefeller Archive Center. Tarrytown NY.

Weindling, Paul. 1997. 'Philanthropy and World Health: The Rockefeller Foundation and the League of Nations Health Organisation'. *Minerva* 35 (3): 269–281.

World Health Organization. 2013. 'Vaccines and Vaccination against Yellow Fever: WHO Position Paper – June 2013'. *Weekly Epidemiological Record* 88 (27): 269–283.

Yergin, Daniel. 1991. *The Prize: The Epic Quest for Oil, Money, and Power.* New York: Simon & Schuster.

Youde, Jeremy. 2013. 'The Rockefeller and Gates Foundations in Global Health Governance'. *Global Society* 27 (2): 139–158.

3 The Ford Foundation

... we must remember that we are invited guests with a role which is usually marginal, interstitial, and indirect ... moral concern is not alone a certain guide to action.

(Bundy 1972, p.viii)

Background and origins

The Ford Foundation dominated philanthropic Foundations for the latter half of the 20th century. From 1950 to 1999 it granted around $10 billion to 9,000 institutions and 100,000 individuals (Arnove and Pined 2007, p.410). Between one quarter and one third of that total went to international development in one form or another. The Ford Foundation has staked a claim as one of the most influential non-governmental development donors of the time. This chapter will argue that, like the Rockefeller Foundation in the interwar period, the Ford Foundation from 1950 under Henry Ford's grandson Henry Ford II, shaped international development both in practice and in theory, at a critical juncture in the Cold War. It had a strong focus on reaching communities with community participation as well as shaping developing country's governments and institutions through its support in planning and building local research capacity, as well as US universities and think tanks in shaping the discourse of development and development studies.

The genesis of the Ford Foundation was quite different to that of the Rockefeller Foundation. While John D. Rockefeller was one of the original 'robber barons' amassing a fortune through Standard Oil (Bridges 1958), he was also a devout Baptist. From the 1880s he spent a significant portion of his wealth on philanthropic causes including the establishment of the Rockefeller Foundation (Fosdick 1952;

Nielsen 1972). On the other hand, Henry Ford senior with his son Edsel, established the Ford Foundation for almost venal purposes, mainly to avoid paying estate taxes. Originally, the Fords wanted to keep the Ford Motor Company as a private family concern so they could maintain control, avoid any scrutiny (it had never been audited), or pay dividends to pesky shareholders. In 1916 they bought all of the outstanding stock in the company to avoid paying dividends to the Dodge brothers after losing a lawsuit brought by them for outstanding dividend payments (Sutton 1987b).

However, with the introduction of an estate tax in 1916, having a family company was not enough to protect their wealth and so the Fords started to look at options to avoid paying this tax when their time came. In the 1930s when the estate tax was increased to 70 per cent on estates above $50 million but with an exemption for charitable trusts, and they were more aware of their own mortality, their hand was forced. They created two classes of Ford Motor Company shares with only 5 per cent of the total holding being actual voting stock held by the family, with the remaining 95 per cent as non-voting stock held by a philanthropic Foundation in their name. The Ford Foundation was founded on January 15, 1936 (Sutton 1987b, p.42)

It was a gift from Henry and Edsel of 125,000 Ford Motor Company shares in 1937 that capitalised the Foundation and provided Henry and Edsel Ford with a mechanism to keep the Ford Motor Company in family hands, come what may (Arnove and Pined 2007; Magat 1979; Sutton 1987b). As MacDonald (1955(2017)) noted:

> The Ford Foundation was a device as simple and efficient as the Model T for perpetuating this privacy in the face of death and taxes [making] the Foundation a pensioner not a partner ... Henry Ford never showed much interest in philanthropy. 'Give the average man something and you are an enemy of him' ... Henry Ford II never heard the Foundation being discussed at home'.
>
> (Macdonald 1955/2017, pp.131–132)

This arrangement also meant that the company could pay lower dividends than its competitors and thus reinvest more in the company, an ironic vindication to Henry Ford's testimony to the 1915 congressional Commission on Industrial Relations looking at foundations where he noted 'I have little use of charities or philanthropies as such' (Arnove and Pined 2007, p.391). This wasn't entirely true as they had opened the Henry Ford Hospital in Detroit in that same year (Rosenfield and

Wimpee 2015), but this was more the exception than the rule of Henry Ford's views of philanthropy.

There was no overarching vision or objectives for the Foundation, or even a clear management structure. This would ultimately prove untenable as the Foundation would have no control or even influence over its own revenue stream (Ford Foundation 1950). The Foundation's activities up until the mid-1940s were an eclectic mix of sometimes idiosyncratic investments in various cultural institutions, mainly in and around Detroit, Michigan. Grants were provided to the Ford Hospital, the Ford Museum, the Detroit Symphony, and the Edison Institute among others (Macdonald 1955(2017); Sutton 1987b; McCarthy 1984; Magat 1979; Bell 1971).

Enter Henry Ford II

By the 1940s Henry Ford had let the Ford Motor Company decline as he became more and more eccentric to the point of madness. This may have driven his son Edsel to despair and an early grave: 'Management had fallen into the hands of a gang of hired thugs under director Harry Burnett long-time head of Ford's private NKVD' (Nielsen 1972, p.78). Something had to be done and Henry Ford's grandson, following a stint in the Navy and the death his father Edsel in 1943, took over the Ford Foundation that year and joined the Ford Motor company in 1945 (Sutton 1987b, Sorensen 1956). When his grandfather father Henry died in 1947, Henry Ford II, together with his mother, took the company over, when it was losing $10 million a month. They revived it out of its moribund state, and on the back of post-war reconstruction made it immensely profitable again.

When the 25-year-old Henry Ford II became President of the Foundation in 1943 he expanded the Board of Trustees as first step to further changes later that decade (Rosenfield and Wimpee 2015). He also developed an overarching vision more about social change that became central to the Foundation both in practice, but also to mark a shift in values of the Foundation from his father and grandfather who chose more local cultural pursuits.[1] The change in the Ford Motor Company fortunes also represented a sea-change for the Foundation. With the Ford Motor Company's return to profitability in the late 1940s, the young Henry Ford II transferred to the Foundation a large amount of Ford stock (very conservatively valued at $480 million ($5 billion in 2019 values)) that Edsel and Henry Senior had bequeathed to the Foundation (Micinski 2017; Sutton 1987b; Bell 1971).

This large injection of capital presented a practical problem for the Foundation, which held 90 per cent of the Ford Motor Company stock, and that was what to do with the increasingly large dividend flows. While the Foundation made no payments in 1947 and 1948, while paying down earlier debts accumulated during Edsel's stewardship, young Henry realised that it had to change its operations and structure to deal with the increased income, and consequent outlays, while respecting the wishes of his father's and grandfather's wills, and other family considerations (McCarthy 1984).

The Gaither report

In the same way as he had revived the Ford Motor Company by bringing the best expertise, Henry Ford II wanted the same to happen with the Foundation. Most importantly he wanted it to have a broad philanthropic purpose to address the social and democratic challenges faced by the US, and the world more broadly (Arnove and Pined 2007). As president of the Foundation, he restructured the Board of Trustees, which until his stewardship from 1943 had been his father, grandfather, and two employees. He brought in expertise from other Foundations as well as academics. In late 1948 he and the board of Trustees commissioned a study on how the Foundation might operate, avoiding giving direction or even suggestions of any particular preferences.

> [His] time to the Foundation … is an interruption to his real job which is running the company. 'I never want to be an advocate. If I got mixed up in all that, I'd never get anything done around here'.
>
> (Macdonald 1955(2017), p.15)

However, the young Henry Ford wanted the Foundation to function well, and not spend too much money on the arts – a marked shift from his father and grandfather. A study was commissioned to make recommendations for a restructuring of the Foundation. It was to be led by Rowan Gaither, who had led the Marshall Plan for the reconstruction of post-war Europe in 1948. Gaither had asked Ford:

> … if he [Ford] was ready to see a majority of the trustees be unrelated to the family or the company, and if the articles of incorporation would be amended so that the board could be self-perpetuating, making members and trustees synonymous. Henry

Ford... expressed the view that the Foundation ought not to represent the interests of a single family but the national interest.

(Sutton 1987b, p.46)

Thus, control of the Foundation moved away from the Ford family and with it the Ford Motor Company, to having only a token representation on the Board of Trustees, and a clear direction to support the 'national interest', however defined. Gainther's committee after a period of extensive consultation (over 1,000 interviews), reported to the Trustees 15 months later in 1950 with a report that:

... became a kind of sacred text, scrutinized for many years by those charged with planning or justifying the Foundation's programs ... The Foundation's declared purpose was to 'advance human welfare,' which was seen as virtually synonymous with democratic ideals.

(Sutton 1987b, p.48)

This new focus recognised the challenges the US faced at the time: both internally in terms of post-war recovery; the conservative forces it faced, such as McCarthyism; as well as the increasingly tense Cold War international environment. The report drew on the language from the Universal Declaration of Human Rights passed by the UN General Assembly only two years earlier:

At its heart this is a belief in the individual and the intrinsic value of human life. Implicit in its concept is the conviction that society must accord all men [sic] equal rights and equal opportunity.

(Ford Foundation 1950, p.7)

That first annual report laid out a set of principles that would endure. The reference to equal opportunity flagged both global poverty work, as well as civil rights in the US, both of which were to dominate its work through the 1960s, while women's rights and gender justice would wait for another nearly 20 years to appear on the Foundation's radar. The Foundation wanted to take a transnational perspective so all issues learned from one context could be taken to another. This way policies could be driven by evidence from demonstration projects funded by Ford that local and national governments could pick up to suit their needs (Arnove and Pined 2007, p.397).

This vision was laid out in five programmes around the broad areas of: peace; democracy; the economy; education; and individual behaviour and human relations. It is not clear why, but programmes on 'individual behaviour' were dropped by the Trustees to be replaced by 'social relations' in 1957. One reason may be that to the trustees it could have smacked of the eugenics work that the Rockefeller Foundation had been involved in pre-war. Later elements of the individual behaviour programme were moved to political science under 'political behaviour' in the 1960s (Hauptmann 2012; Roelofs 2003). The Foundation was to be run by staff with the Trustees having oversight of broad policy and direction, but not specific programmes. Henry Ford II resigned as president in 1950, to be a reluctant Chair of the Board of Trustees until 1956, when he stepped down. However, he remained on the Board for another 20 years, well into the 1970s, serving over 30 years as a Trustee of the Ford Foundation.

There was no mention of the Ford Motor Company or the Ford family in the Gainther report, and it was understood that under the leadership of Henry Ford II, the Foundation would move to being independent of the family. Henry was to be more an 'ambassador at large' rather than a representative of the family or the company. He bit his tongue on his views on the direction the Foundation was taking until his retirement in 1976, when he made some pertinent parting points in a leaked letter to the Board that caused some controversy (Magat 1979; Ford 1976). Outgoing President McGeorge Bundy drily noted at the time that: '... it is no more than a marginal irony that what has most clearly underlined the Foundation's independence is his [Ford's] own decision to resign from our Board of Trustees with some pungent parting advice' (Bundy 1977; Ford 1976). The 'advice' was around what Ford saw as 'biting the hand that feeds' in terms of what he saw as the Foundation's invisible relationship with capitalism in its programs.

> ... the foundation is a creature of capitalism. [But] it is hard to discern recognition of this fact in anything the foundation does ... I'm not playing the role of the hard-headed tycoon who thinks all philanthropoids are socialists and all university professors are communists. I'm just suggesting to the trustees and the staff that the system that makes the foundation possible, very probably is worth preserving.
>
> (Ford 1976, p.vi)

Any number of Foundation funded business schools then and now would probably disagree that there was no attention to capitalism in the Ford Foundation's work.

The renewed Ford Foundation: achieving autonomy

Despite Henry's own silence, the Foundation continued to be directly challenged from senior staff of the Ford Motor Company and other Ford family members in Detroit. They believed, with their share-holding, they still had some say in the direction and work of the Foundation. They felt there was a reputational risk to the company name with the Foundation's work (Nielsen 1972). Henry Ford II was well aware of the issue that the Foundation's Ford Motor Company assets were controlled by the Ford family through the 10 per cent that was the voting stock. This was untenable for an independent Board of Trustees, as they had no say in dividend flows, and also in the eyes of regulators, who saw the relationship between the Foundation and the Company as being too close, and a reminder of Congress's concerns with the Rockefeller Foundation some 40 years earlier.

Considerable effort was spent on working on a sensible way of divesting this stock, which in 1951 was valued by the company for reporting purposes, at \$417 million (\$4.1 billion in 2019 dollars) which was an unrealistic low estimate given the size of the dividends it was paying to the Foundation. The true value would not be known until the company was floated in 1956 (Sutton 1987b, p.52).[2] The trustees could only spend about one tenth of these dividends on their current programmes, and: 'The Internal Revenue Bureau was becoming restive' (Macdonald 1955(2017), p.140), as were politicians.

> In 1949 … it [the Ford Foundation] shot up from a good-sized institution to a gigantic one [and faced] the usual horrendous edifice of charges including un-Americanism, subversion, egg-headism, and general left deviationism … propped up by the usual mixture of midget quarter truths, mammoth innuendos, and cosmic implications. Perplexing to the shades of Andrew Carnegie and John D Rockefeller [who] got plenty of unfriendly attention … from precisely the opposite quarter.
>
> (Macdonald 1955(2017), p.21)

In 1952 the Select Committee to Investigate Tax-Exempt Founda-tions and Comparable Organizations was established, and while it focussed on a McCarthy type investigation into un-American activ-ities, it did put the Ford Foundation under the spotlight because of its civil rights work. This 'infuriated the Ford family in Detroit' and caused concern with the Ford Motor Company, which was experien-cing intermittent boycotts of its cars, mainly in the South and parts of

the West of the US (Nielsen 1972, p.83). These boycotts were to continue well into the 1960s (Ford Foundation 1966). In 1954 Congress-
man Reece investigated the financial activities of Foundations and
recommended:

> banning foundations from operating in perpetuity. In addition,
> suggested restricting tax-exempt status against foundations invested
> heavily in business securities.
>
> (Micinski 2017, p.1316)

While the report was ridiculed and rejected as anti-communist hys-
teria, the focus on the Foundation's Ford Motor Company's investments did give pause for thought to the Foundation's Trustees, who
were preparing to sell down the Foundation's Ford Motor Company
stock.

Divesting the stock on this scale was a slow process and relied on
the Ford Motor Company itself being floated as well, to provide
something for the buyers of the stock to control. The sale did not
really get under way until late 1955 and early 1956 when it sold 10.2
million shares together with voting rights (Nielsen 1972, p.87). This
sale with an initial public offering from the Ford Motor Company
provided a clear message that the Foundation was no longer a way to
keep the Ford Motor Company in the family, being nearly one quarter
of the Foundation's stock in the Ford Motor Company (Magat 1979,
p.32): '... realizing $641 million, and it promptly gave away $548 million [$5.2b in 2019 $] in an unprecedented largesse to American
universities, liberal arts colleges, and hospitals' (Sutton 1987a, p.viii).

These grants were aimed to make the Foundation 'better and more
favourably known' (Sutton 1987b, p.83), and were on an unprecedented scale: $550 million to 600 private accredited four year colleges;
$200 million for faculty salaries; $198 million to 3,500 non-profit
hospitals; and $90 million to 45 medical schools (Nielsen 1972, p.87).
'Henry Ford II said let's make the number an uneven number ... so it
will look like we have considered the matter carefully'. (p.88). This
give-away also represented a large reduction in the Foundation's capital base and raised the question of the longevity of the Foundation,
which Trustees had to confront ten years later as the capital base was
further eroded by financial crises, and whether the Foundation would
or should operate in perpetuity (Ford Foundation 1950, 1966a).

This largesse led to a rapid change in public sentiment to the Ford
Foundation from both within and outside the Ford Motor Company,
and the beginning of a long relationship of supporting higher

education. As Nielsen puts it, the Foundation became a '... a banking partner to higher education' (Nielsen 1972, p.92). It was also one of the few higher education grant programs that did not have any strong conditions as to the direction and shape of research, but there may have been implicit ones. As Laski noted in 1930 when foundations began funding university research:

> ... the foundations do not control simply because, in the simple and direct sense of the word, there is no need for them to do so. They have only to indicate the immediate direction of their minds for the whole university world to discover that it always meant to gravitate swiftly to that angle of the intellectual compass.
>
> (Laski 1930, p.174)

The discourse on international development from these Foundation supported institutions has always had a liberal democratic bent to them (Micinski 2017). This largesse also had the spin-off effect of improving the reputation of the Foundation's international development programme. The sale of stock, however, was a relatively slow process and it took another ten years or more for the Foundation to divest itself of 70 per cent of its Ford Motor Company stock and reinvest the proceeds in over 100 different stock holdings. This was important to make it clear that the Ford family could have little control over the Foundation through its stock holdings (Bell 1971). Divesting, however, did not totally protect the family name and the Ford Motor Company (Ford Foundation 1966). In the mid-1960s Portugal boycotted Ford cars in its government fleet as a protest over the Ford Foundation support for the FRELIMO the independence movement (Bell 1971, p.475).

There was also the issue of government scrutiny. In 1963 an Informal Advisory Congressional Committee on Foundations identified six problems with foundations including:

> ... self-dealing; delay in [paying] benefits to charity; foundation involvement in business; family use of foundations to control corporate or other property; financial transactions unrelated to charitable functions; and, broadening of foundation management.
>
> (Micinski 2017, p.1317)

These issues were to be the basis of the tax reform act of 1969, which had the effect of a massive increase in administration expenses as defensive mechanisms against Congress and the regulators. The proportion spent on administration rose from 2.3 per cent in 1966 to 22.3 per cent in 1978 (Micinski 2017, p.1318).

Holding on to Ford Motor Company stock also had a number of other implications. The mid-1960s were the most lucrative terms of the Foundations stock holding and the generosity of their grants, because of the profitability of the Ford Motor Company. In GDP adjusted terms the $3.3 billion asset base at the time was equivalent to $45 billion in 2000, not far short of the Gates Foundation in equivalence of scale of operations. Through that period the value of the grants was often double the income, so the issue remained that any turn of the stock market would leave the Foundation vulnerable.

McGeorge Bundy, as Foundation President from the late 1960s, oversaw a series of large cuts to wind back the exuberance of the early 1960s, when the leadership was less concerned with the notions of perpetuity. Grants in 1964 were 140 per cent of income (Macdonald 1955(2017); Rosenfield and Wimpee 2015). 'If Ford was making a "big bang" it looked to be exploding itself to do so' (Sutton 1987a, p.xvii). Bundy wanted to maintain, if not increase, the size of the foundation's asset base. The cuts he instituted, mainly to the US university programmes, were not enough, and the oil crisis and its financial knock-on effects of the 1970s saw further cuts as the asset base fell below $2 billion. By 1979 annual grant expenditure was a low $108 million compared to $300 million in the early 1960s. The overseas programmes took its fair share of cuts, but grants directed to basic needs in food production and population were protected (Sutton 1987a). From 1974–78 the staff numbers and programme grants were halved as a result of this 'structural adjustment' (Rosenfield and Wimpee 2015).

As Bundy noted a decade later, the exuberance of the 1960s placed the Foundation in the horns of a dilemma, so that Bundy spent most of his ten years as president trying to manage the dilemma '... if we had been larger in 1969 and our record of giving less generous, the congressional reaction would have been much worse' (Bundy 1978, p.ix). The 1969 legislation regulating Foundations that Bundy was referring to did not hobble the Ford Foundation in any significant way: the rule that disbursements be 6 per cent of the asset base, or all of the dividends, whichever was higher, had been well exceeded through the 1960s. The main issue the Foundation had with the new regulations was a 4 per cent excise tax on all disbursements, which did hurt it. By 1978 this tax had been cut back to 2 per cent, the figure the Foundations had wanted from the outset (Bundy 1978, p.vii)

It was not until 1974 that the Foundation's final stock in the Ford Motor Company was sold (Magat 1979, p.76). From 1970 to 1972 as part of the divestment strategy, there was an internal discussion of providing large grantees Ford Motor Company stock in lieu of cash grants. This was in part to avoid paying the 4 per cent excise tax on share sales and dividends (Dressner 1971, 1972; Ford Foundation 1970). The condition of any such grant was that the grantees had to hold the stock for five years, thus raising a broader ethical issue of providing grants in the form of volatile company stocks that had to be held for five years.

This created an additional problem for the international programme which was also reluctant to be part of this plan, as having development partners holding Ford Motor Company stock was a reputational risk to the partners (Hertz 1970a). For example, in the Middle East, where the Ford Motor Company had a plant in Israel, there was an Arab boycott of Ford cars in place (Hertz 1970b). Second, having stock in a company with strong business cycle effects on its income did not make a lot of sense as it transferred the risk to the development partner. There had been two crashes in Ford stock the Foundation had to deal with, one in 1966 and one in 1971. As a result of these concerns there is no record of an international programme or its partners taking up the offer of Ford stock. The US Universities with their own, often very large endowments, were most able to take up these offers.

Even when the Ford stock was finally sold the Foundation still had issues with its endowment base and income stream. It was further hit hard later in the 1970s financial crises when more than car companies were hit by hard times. The 1970s was a decade in which neither stocks nor bonds yielded returns much above the rate of inflation. The only option for the Foundation were further cuts to limit any new commitments (Bundy 1974). In the 1980s the cuts continued under the new president, Franklin Thomas, when there was another round of cuts to programmes and staff which was less gradual than Bundy's, and therefore more traumatic. The unexpected cut to 20 senior programme officers in May 1981 became known as the Mother's Day Massacre (Rosenfield and Wimpee 2015). But this put the Foundation on a sound financial footing and Thomas was able to increase the international programmes throughout his presidency.

It was also the first 20 years of regulatory and sometimes financial turmoil where the Ford Foundation made its mark on international development. It faced a number of challenges in how to drive its programmes particularly in the support of governments that the Gaither Report and the 1950s programme focussed on.

Supporting governments

In the 1950s, supporting governments with Foundation grants was a core activity. This was to change in the 1960s and 1970s when the 1969 regulation required that the grantees have similar status to the Foundation in domestic law. This resulted in a shift in Ford from supporting governments to supporting human rights and other NGOs. '[The] Foundation gave 15% of international grants directly to foreign governments in its first decade of existence, but by 2001 was cut to just under 2%' (Micinski 2017, p.1305). The caveat is that the Foundation continued to spend quite a bit on government research institutes, based presumably on the argument that they had a level of autonomy from their host government.

This shift away from supporting government was not only driven by the regulators but the Foundation itself. The 1960s and the war in Vietnam saw a public disillusionment with foreign aid supporting Third World governments. This was around the time of a number of Latin American military coups: Brazil 1964; Chile and Uruguay 1973; and Argentina 1976. Also, in the 1960s and 1970s domestic issues around civil rights began to take precedence over global issues. As a result, the Foundation moved to implement its own community development projects abroad as a defensive mechanism against hostile scrutiny of any relations it had with foreign governments, lest Ford be accused of supporting communism, on the one hand, or military dictatorships on the other. This shift away from supporting government was a fundamental philosophical move away from the Gaither committee report of 1950 and the Foundation's early years:

> Core to the Ford Foundation's development philosophy at the time was the idea that governments are the key drivers for change in society. Governments had vast resources, much larger than a private foundation, and the authority to spear head ambitious development projects. The foundation's role could be to prove the effectiveness of certain projects and hand-off these initiatives to governments.
>
> (Micinski 2017, p.1309)

The proportion spent domestically likewise increased, with Ford's foreign spend falling from around one third in the early 1950s to around 15–20 per cent for a period. It was the 17-year presidency of Frederick A. Thomas through the 1980s into the 1990s that saw the foreign aid budget restored to around one third of the total programme, and by 2003 it was closer to 40 per cent. This boost was relatively short lived, and by the 2010s a renewed focus on civil rights in the US saw international grants fall to around 20 per cent of the total and less than $100 million per year (Ford Foundation Grants Database, accessed Feb 2020)[3].

Re-imagining social sciences

A distinctive focus of the Ford Foundation was in the social sciences, particularly in US higher education and policy. While the Rockefeller Foundation's major focus was in the biological sciences, the Ford Foundation was firmly focused on the social sciences. They saw the role of involving society more broadly as a more direct way of advancing democracy and staving off communist or left-wing influences. In all of their advocacy and policy work the Foundation adopted moderate approaches and eschewed more radical action. This was as much evidenced in the domestic civil rights programme as well as in international programmes, as Marquez (2020) found with the Latino programs in the US in the 1960s. There is an argument that the Foundation was pulled leftwards by the social movements of the 1960s:

> ... as the Sixties wore on and the values of the New Left spread through American society, an activist spirit entered the Foundation that pulled it away from the study group's original vision of solving the world's problems through scientific knowledge.
>
> (Sutton 1987a, p.xv)

This political influence resulted in tensions and occasional push back. In 2004 the American Civil Liberties Union declined a $1.3 million grant from the Ford Foundation and returned $68,000 due to conditions placed on its advocacy following the 9/11 terrorist attacks on New York. According to Barker, the Ford Foundation had a history of steering the direction and strengths of social issues advocacy, and in doing so creating a wedge between groups and their supporters (2008, p.18). It is hard, however, to argue that this was as widespread as Barker argues given the sheer scale of the work. The idea of grantees declining grants or returning them, however, was also unimaginable for the Ford Foundation (Edwards 2019). Small NGOs can decline smaller grants as they generally diversify their income sources (Kilby 2006), but the size of Ford Foundation grants generally overwhelmed an NGO's funding base, and so made it much harder to decline let alone return the offer in later years.

International programmes

While the Gainther committee report of 1950 did not explicitly call for the establishment of an international programme, the four areas of focus implied a strong international component of the work under the heading of Peace, as an '... agency which promised to make meaningful contributions to world peace' (Sutton 1987b, p.49). Driven by the idea that 'more knowledge promotes peace' (Bell 1971, p.471), a knowledge focus would soon include overseas development, international training and research, and international affairs (Magat 1979). The overseas development work meshed well with President Truman's Point Four programme for increased development cooperation as part of his Cold War security agenda released the year before (Micinski 2017; Wood 1986; Kilby 2017). There were four sub-areas of activity of the Foundation's Peace programme:

1   the mitigation of tensions which threaten world peace;
2   the development among peoples of the world of the understanding and conditions essential to permanent peace;
3   the improvement and strengthening of the United Nations and its associated international agencies; and
4   the improvement of the structure and procedures by which the United States government and private American groups participate in world affairs.

(Bell 1971, p.468)

This gave Hoffman, as the Foundation's new president, plenty of ammunition to prosecute a programme to rapidly expand its international profile, particularly under points one and two. 'The Foundation was thus in declaration and perception essentially committed to international purposes' (Sutton 1987b, p.49). In its first ten years the Ford Foundation devoted some $500 million (~$4.5 billion in 2019) to development assistance. International training and research between 1952 and 1966 amounted to $240 million given to US universities for training and research in non-Western area studies, or what has also became known as development studies (Bell 1971, pp.468–469). This was either directly funded by the Foundation or through Foundation supported bodies such as the Social Sciences Research Council. There was an ideological flavour to this work: for example, the way funding was targeted tended to move political science away from ideology and theory as such, to examine the political behaviour and public opinions of voters and others. There seemed to be an assumption that liberal democracy was a given:

Ford's program gave academics from across the social sciences (including political science) strong incentives to join the effort of figuring out what behavioralism was and how they might help build it.

(Hauptmann 2012, p.163)

The Foundation also developed elite knowledge networks with countries ranging from China to Poland in an attempt to influence their communist ideology (Huo and Parmar 2019; Czernecki 2013). This programme ran into difficulties when the CIA was not only instrumental in the formation of organisations such as the Asia Foundation, but also saw the students of Ford Foundation education programmes as potential agents for the CIA (Roelofs 2007). Ford Foundation presidents, Gaither and Heald over a decade, complained to the CIA that it threated the integrity and reputation of the Foundation and its programmes. These programmes were not only an important part of the Foundation's work, but also of US foreign policy (Berman 1983). In the 1960s the Foundation rejected overtures from the Asia Foundation to replace the $8 million of CIA funding it had been receiving, after the Asia Foundation's CIA links were made public. It was seen as a risk to the Ford Foundation's credibility, especially in countries such as India where it had a very large programme and the Indian government was well aware of CIA activities within its borders (Bell 1968a, 1968b; Bresnan and Edwards 1968). A decade later the Foundation was still fending off accusations it was channelling CIA funding (Magat 1978). There was no suggestion there was direct funding, but there may have been CIA funding to some Ford partners, which the Ford Foundation was unaware of, but was caught up in through 'guilt by association'.

Policy priorities

How the original vision of the Ford Foundation with its foreign policy focus was to be implemented in a programmatic sense led to vigorous debates through the early 1950s. In the beginning there were three distinct international programmes: International Training and Research (ITR); International Affairs; and Overseas Development (Bell 1971). The focus on peace was a clear part of all of these, but this raised the question of whether to focus on Europe, the front line of the Cold War, or alternatively focus on the newly independent countries, such as India, Indonesia, and Pakistan, which could be useful proxies for Cold War rivalry between the US and the Soviet

Union, and later China, through their respective national development cooperation programs (Kilby 2017).

In practice both were funded for the first few years at least: the East European Fund, while a favourite of the Foundation leadership, was unable to clearly identify appropriate programmes of research for implementation. It ended up funding refugee programs through UNHCR ($2.9 million) and indirectly through the East Europe Fund ($3.8 million), as well as working with East Europeans refugees in the US, who were having difficulty settling in (Sutton 1987b). Exceptions included an academic exchange programme with Poland in the late 1950s, which was a great success in strengthening the discipline of sociology in Polish academia, but as a propaganda coup, in moving Polish politics away from Soviet sponsorship, it was much less successful (Czernecki 2013).

The Atlantic Institute funded by the Foundation was also a way of maintaining a strong diplomatic and business community between the US and Western Europe in the early 1960s (Scott-Smith 2014). These, however, were difficult to spread to other countries, and lacked the drive and programme opportunities of a focus on developing countries. The third objective 'the improvement and strengthening of the United Nations and its associated international agencies' had very little support from the Trustees who, even in those early years, were sceptical of the effectiveness of the UN, and the programme lapsed except for support for UNHCR and UNESCO in the refugee space (Magat 1979; Sutton 1987b).[4]

The early success of the international programme came from targeting important regions where there was a willing recipient and a high level of Cold War contestation. The obvious candidates were in South Asia and the Middle East, where they would be argued as promoting peace through 'the relief of tension in underdeveloped areas'. These would receive nearly $13 million in 1952 alone (Sutton 1987b, p.66). India was an obvious favourite due to its sheer size but also it was seen by Foundation President Hoffman (with a nod to Winston Churchill) as the 'underbelly of China' (Berman 1983, p.56)

This rapid expansion in international development funding by Hoffman, was driven by his experience as a former administrator of the Marshall Plan (1948–1950), and an internationalist who saw a role for the Foundation in complementing both the Marshall Plan and Truman's Point Four programme of economic cooperation. The Foundation would fund technical assistance in support of governments, but at arm's length from the US government (Micinski 2017). 'To Hoffman … international problems could yield to the kind of constructive effort and optimism that he liked to apply to other problems' (Sutton 1987b, p.54). He was also supported by the government, for example McGhee, a US senior state department official, in a letter to Hoffman, noted '... that help and guidance is often better received, and more effective if tendered by private interests rather than through government channels' (McGhee 1951, p.1).

Hoffman was supported by a team that included Robert Hutchins his provocative highbrow lieutenant (Sutton 1987a; Nielsen 1972, p.82), who expanded the programme and soon had officers on site developing programmes in India, Pakistan, Lebanon, Indonesia, and Burma. This rapid growth in the program 'spooked' the Board of Trustees who thought Hoffman's and Hutchins' ideas on this expansion, as well as supporting the UN, were a waste of time and money. This inevitably led to clashes between Hoffman and Ford, while Hutchins continued to lobby the Trustees for more support to the UN, in part to improve the image of the US globally: 'America, in spite of the will to peace that characterises its people, could easily become a menace. Some foreigners seem to believe she is so now' (Hutchins 1953, p.1)

Hoffman was absent at a critical juncture in the life of the Foundation, campaigning for presidential candidate Dwight Eisenhower, and he left decision-making to Hutchins with his almost contemptuous attitude to the Trustees (Nielsen 1972). This was happening during the Korean War, which heralded a change in public sentiment to: '... one of fear and from progressivism to reaction. Ford Foundation became a favourite target for militant anti-communists' and the first of many rounds of public boycotts of Ford cars started to occur (Nielsen 1972, pp.82–83). The rift between senior management and the Board of Trustees could not continue and the upshot was the sacking of Hoffman by Henry Ford II as Chair of the Board in 1952, after he had only spent 22 months in the job as president (Sutton 1987b).

In his brief time at the helm Hoffman had set the direction for the international programme that was to continue. 'No one of the great foundations since then has approached the depth and variety of Ford's international activities' (Sutton 1987b, p.74). Hoffman's influence over the international programme was greater than the much larger domestic programme. Key to this approach were the relationships with governments including the US government: by 1955 US diplomats and partner governments were paving the way for the Foundation's overseas programmes to come to their countries, as President Eisenhower 'embraced the Foundation's direct involvement with foreign governments' (Nemchenok 2009, p.262). This 'embrace' was to last for another ten years, as noted above, before sentiment turned against supporting governments in the mid-1960s. By the time the Foundation celebrated its 30th anniversary in 1980, $1.7 billion had been spent on international programmes with around $1 billion spent in the Third World, with the rest supporting the international programmes of US universities (McCarthy 1984).

India programme

The focus of the Foundation in the early 1950s was very much with the governments of the Global South, such as Pakistan and India, which were the recipients of the first large grants in 1951 of over $2 million (Micinski 2017). They were obvious candidates: newly independent; in tension if not outright war with each other; and sitting within the Soviet Union's (and China's) sphere of influence. Initial funding to India went to agricultural institutes, and a memorial fund for Gandhi; and in Pakistan as support for a women's association (Micinski 2017). The plan was to also have staff in place by 1952 to substantially expand the programme in India, Pakistan, and elsewhere by 1953 (Sutton 1987b). Hoffman visited New Delhi in early 1951, 'announcing a new, broadly international focus for the Ford Foundation's philanthropic endeavours to halt the feared advance of Communism' (Loveridge 2017, p.61).

This program had a 'dual rhetoric of liberal humanitarianism and technocratic social engineering' (Sackley 2012, p.234). While the Foundation headquarters may have had a vision of scientific knowledge and some of the work with agriculture may come into this, the staff were more pragmatic, and worked with the Indian government on its own priorities: community development; public administration; population control; and urban planning. Douglas Ensminger, the first Ford Foundation representative in India, exemplified this pragmatism: his background was in rural sociology and ten years' work with the Department of Agriculture's land grant college programme, and so he was very familiar with community development approaches to agriculture. He also drew on his former colleagues from the Tennessee Valley Authority, who brought a much broader focus to agricultural extension and community development, rather than that of the White House or State Department (Sackley 2012).

Ensminger also had a sharp political analysis of the relationship between India and the US. He noted in a memo about India relations with China and the Soviet Union that given 'India's psychosis about colonialism, and the US psychosis about communism', political equality between India and the US was central to the US relationship (Ensminger 1955). Needless to say this was not ready to happen under Eisenhower in the 1950s nor, in particular, under the Johnson administration ten years later.[5] Ensminger was also aware of the opportunities offered by the Soviet Union and the importance of the US in countering them: an example of which was training Indian engineers in the US (Ensminger 1956; Ford Foundation 1957).

Ensminger set up the Ford Foundation in Delhi with the intention of not only being a friend to India, but also as a devoted ally to India's first prime minister Jawaharlal Nehru (Sackley 2012, p.234). The Foundation took on projects that were too sensitive domestically for the Indian government: it was instrumental in setting up the Planning Commission as a centre of power for Nehru to bolster himself against attacks from left wing parties. Not least of these was the Communist Party of India, which was a trenchant critic of the Foundation's community development programme. It saw the programme as competition to its own local political activism, and never accepted the Foundation's 'pose of neutrality' (Sackley 2012; Macdonald 1955 (2017), p.235). It was the community development programme under its various iterations which was the most far reaching in those early years, despite its flaws, as it ultimately led to the Green Revolution and enabled it to succeed.

The community development programme in India had its origins in the work of an American ex-Army town planner Albert Mayer, at Etawah in Uttar Pradesh (Bang and Suresh 1952), and that of Surendra Dey's work with a refugee community in Nikheri, West Punjab, both in 1948.

> The project garnered attention from national and international press, quickly drawing the interest of American philanthropic organisations and international development experts eager to test their theories of modernisation and generate a replicable model of rural development.
>
> (Loveridge 2017, p.57)

The Foundation's President Hoffman visited both sites in 1951, and the Ford Foundation together with the US government proposed a massive scaling up of the programmes both in size within the two districts, and across both states and further (Perkins 1990; Loveridge 2017). An initial Ford Foundation grant of $1.5 million in 1951 was the first instalment in this scaling up, to train 6000 agricultural extension workers to implement new farming techniques (Lerner 2018;

Perkins 1990; Kilby 2019; Loveridge 2017). In early 1952, an agreement leveraging off the Ford Foundation work was signed between the US Technical Cooperation Administration (TCA) and the government of India. The US government provided $50 million and the government of India more than matched that funding. This had the effect of staving off the foreign exchange hungry need for new technical infrastructure such as irrigation facilities for increased agricultural productivity (Perkins 1990, p.13).

The Ford Foundation's work soon expanded to Indian agricultural colleges as the British colonial input withdrew, which complemented the Rockefeller Foundation's work with universities. Partnerships were brokered by Ensminger with land grants universities, to help build the local extension services. The village training work was largely led by staff from India's own agricultural universities, polytechnics, and government ministries who made up the bulk of the rural extension trainers.

> Contingents from the Ford Foundation and the TCA remained on-hand to observe and periodically offer lectures on rural life, public health, and the workings of government in the United States.
>
> (Loveridge 2017, p.63)

Between 1951 and 1956 over $16 million was spent in India with half going to community level projects. Over time the programmes' successes waned, and by 1957 the focus had shifted away from agriculture to village welfare, becoming excessively bureaucratic (Loveridge 2017), and as Bang and Suresh (1952) anticipated, very much top down. In the 1960s, however, these extension projects were resurrected with a sharper focus on agriculture and food security and the Ford Foundation with the Rockefeller Foundation introduced new technology as part of the extension work (Ford Foundation 1960a, 1960b, 1967).

This work in India was important in a number of ways. It was led by the priorities of the recipient government, and India was very much interested in extension-led agricultural development rather than technology, something that would come later in the 1960s. Second, it was also in collaboration with both the Rockefeller Foundation and the US government. This was a collaboration that was to continue in the agriculture sector through the 1950s to the 1970s and beyond. The big issue in that extension programme, which persists into the 2010s, was the failure to reach women farmers:

Community development's engagement of village women represented a means to the end of ensuring India's food security
[through nutrition programs], but [it] remained largely silent
regarding the education ... of women as agricultural experts or
primary cultivators themselves.

(Loveridge 2017, p.65)

The positive effect of the programme was that Green Revolution technologies were taken up more strongly in those places where the community development and extension programme had been carried out a
decade earlier and still continued (Kilby 2019; Loveridge 2017). When
a similar programme was tried in Iran it was a complete failure, largely
due to the indifference of the Iranian government, with the US government pursuing a foreign policy agenda aimed at keeping the Shah in
place rather than empowering the peasants (Nemchenok 2009).

Ensminger's influence in India waned in the 1960s as bureaucratic
and political resistance to the power of the Planning Commission
grew, together with a personal animosity over his influence on Nehru.
Likewise, the Ford Foundation Head Office in New York was pushing
back against Ensminger and his support for the Indian government.
For example, Gaither as president proposed research on communist
influence (in India) under the Foundation's Asia studies program with
US Universities. Ensminger objected that this would politicise the
Ford Foundation in India, and he used the Planning Commission to
wind this programme back, to be less ideological in its focus (Sackley
2012, p.245). There was more pressure against funding governments
when President Heald in a memo to Hill his vice-president for international programs, refers to the '... undesirability of making grants to
foreign governments' (Heald 1963), despite that being the focus of the
programme for the previous ten years. There were also hints from
head office for Ensminger to move on from the early 1960s despite, or
perhaps because of, his best efforts to keep head office from
'meddling' (Isaacs 1958).

So, the writing was on the wall for the autonomy of the Indian
programme:

... by the 1960s this began to change as New York became more
bureaucratic and pressured India to narrow the plethora of projects and focus on population and food which left it vulnerable to
criticism in India and part of a Third World critique of the west
'academic colonialism'.

(Sackley 2012, p.236)

There was also an ideological shift under Heald in which the emphasis was on foreign expertise rather than local capacity:

> ... [so] the egalitarian emphasis largely disappears and is replaced by a managerial approach, emphasizing the competence of leaders, self-confidence in the Foundation's ability to define problems, and in the applicability of western techniques.
>
> (Martin 1971, p.23)

After Nehru's death in 1964 the Foundation lost access to Indian policy makers, and when Ensminger retired in 1970, the Foundation's Delhi office was reorganised with funding shifting from government to NGOs, in line with what was happening elsewhere. In the 1970s the focus on support for the government management training institutes and the University of Delhi continued, but with fewer foreign (read US) experts. In the 1980s, gender and human rights, a particular focus of the incoming Ford Foundation president, became a particular focus.

By the 2000s the Ford Foundation began to look like any other international NGO, and its special status with the Indian government was certainly over when in 2015 it ran afoul of the Modi government, which was very critical of liberal NGOs, both locally and internationally (Aurora 2015). It sought to have the Ford Foundation expelled or put on very tight restrictions, and it was only some behind the scenes diplomatic work by senior US political figures that the Foundation was allowed to remain in India relatively unrestricted (Mitra and Srivas 2016; Mallet 2015).

China

The Ford Foundation had an interest in China from the early 1950s when it was isolated from the West. The Foundation initially funded Chinese studies programme at US universities as well as some work in Taiwan and Hong Kong to broaden their 'ethnocentric approach' to education (Staples 1969; Finkelstein 1969). It was also clear that this work was a prelude to work in mainland China, to the point that concerns were raised that Taiwan should not be seen as an 'ante-room to something larger' (Passin 1968, p.1). In the early 1970s more work was done with the China studies programmes at US universities with $40 million provided through the 1960s. In 1966 the Foundation set up the National Committee on China US Relations to brief Congress and others, and in 1971 the Foundation sought visas for a visit by senior staff (Ford Foundation 1971). This coincided with the very public visit of the US table tennis team, and the much less public visits by Secretary of State Henry Kissinger also in 1971, as the first step in the thaw of relations with the China and the US, all leading to US President Richard Nixon's visit early the following year.

For the Ford Foundation, it was not until 1979 that they got their foot in the door, and a cooperation visit occurred and a programme of exchanges over a number of years was developed (Robinson 1979). These exchanges were so successful that between:

> 1978 and 2008, 1.3 million Chinese studied abroad, 37 per cent of them to the US; around 370,000 returned home and took up leading positions in reformist research institutes.
>
> (Huo and Parmar 2019, p.9)

In 1980 other specific programmes were being planned, such as a remote agriculture in Xian (Ford Foundation 1980). These exchanges led to the development of knowledge networks, which came out of the Chinese studies centres developed in the US from the 1960s. Huo and Parmer (2019) argue that it was these networks that shifted Chinese economic policy and thinking away from Marxist economics to neo-classical economics, as a way to advance US hegemony:

> [knowledge networks] informal but semi-official in practice, independent of but authorized by both states, were fundamental to China's shift to a market-oriented economy. In the process, Ford (alongside and in cooperation with the World Bank, among others) helped re-construct the very identity of Chinese economists into neo-classical as opposed to Marxist, within a new scientific community.
>
> (Huo and Parmar 2019, p.3)

This 'conspiracy theory', however, breaks down when it became clear that it was China that wanted to modernise, and therefore it was taking as much as the West could offer in terms of funding as well as knowledge. By the late 2010s Western governments were complaining about the success of this strategy, accusing China of intellectual property theft. China never fully adopted neo-classical economics but rather developed neo-structuralism, a form of Keynesianism, through which Lin and others, with their World Bank experience, helped in the re-shaping of not only China's economy, but also that of its neighbours. It demonstrated that countries could be economically successful, at least up to a point under authoritarian systems, and a liberal democracy was not a necessary element (Lin 2011).

To the extent to which Ford was complicit in a US hegemonic process, it was less than successful. While the Foundation certainly wanted China to be open, it is less certain that the Foundation wanted to be an active participate in a blatant push for US hegemony. I argue, as with India, when the Ford Foundation supported India's economic policies and its opposition to the Johnson administration pressure, that Ford was more focussed on China's needs directly, rather than the political system *per se*.

Population

The population programmes of the 1950s and 1960s, in contrast to Ensminger's work in India, is one that is a case of poorer judgment of the Foundation, and arguably arose from pressure, in this case from John D. Rockefeller III. The population programmes of the time had much the same elements of other programmes which was that technology could lead social engineering to reduce family size particularly of Indian families (the focus at the time) regardless of context. For the first 20 years the focus was on reducing family sizes, through often coercive practices of birth control, common in both India, and in China under its one child policy. In the case of India the government was funded by the Foundation, for example, a $5 million grant in 1962 to the Indian government for 'family planning' work (Ford Foundation 1962). These were top down and often (en)forced programmes, such as the forced sterilisation programme of the early 1970s (Banerji 1976). This created a massive backlash against the Indian government, and the bad publicity was one reason for the move of the Ford Foundation away from supporting government programmes more generally. From the 1970s the Foundation shifted in its focus from the language of 'birth control' to 'family planning', and then to 'reproductive health'. There was also a move from clinical interventions with large camps and campaigns, to rural health with extension services focussing on a broader set of public health issues, including nutrition, access to schooling, and other structural issues (Caldwell and Caldwell 1986). Paradoxically, 50 years later in a moment of history seeming to repeating itself, the Gates Foundation has been caught up in a similar controversy in its own population programme in India, and the use of Depo-Provera implants (Wilson 2018).

The Ford Foundation in the 2000s

The first two decades of the 21st century are quite different from the first 20 years of the re-formed Foundation from 1950. The 1950s and 1960s were filled with optimism and the self-belief that the Foundation was a major player in international development, supporting government planning processes as well as research in key issues such as food security, community development, town planning and population; and a key if not a major player in higher education and civil rights in the US. By the 2000s, even though the Foundation had recovered from the declining revenues of the 1970s and 1980s, it did not have the same relationship with governments, nor did it want to. The population work had moved into a broader agenda in women's rights and access, and the agricultural work had been largely completed at least at an institutional research level. Spending on international development had reached a peak in the late 1990s, but in the 2000s it started to decline.

For a period under Lius Ubiñas (2007–2012) the Foundation shifted away from its rights-based agenda, and moved to a business-based model, an emphasis on individual entrepreneurialism and the free market, with performance being a key indicator of grantee success: gone were the days of large-scale involvement and leadership in global issues of social justice. The period also marked a steady decline in the proportion of funding going to international programmes. The Ubiñas period was not a success and he served only one term. His successor Darren Walker returned the Foundation to a single-minded focus on inequality, and returned it to the civil rights and social justice roots of McGeorge Bundy and Franklin Thomas. While Walker may be part of the East Coast elite, he was not born into it, coming from a poor single parent black family in the South, where he gained a life lesson of a marginalised community, and a beneficiary of the 1960s 'head start' programme to provide opportunities for poor children. This drove his work with black communities in Harlem and his work with the large foundations, first with Rockefeller and later Ford.

Walker increased the proportion of unrestricted grants and institutional support to cover the running costs of partners. The GOS (general operating support) proportion of grants shifted from 25 per cent to 70 per cent from 2015 to 2019 and overheads to projects from 10 to 20 per cent (Pennington 2020). This was a move back to the philosophy of the 1950s and 1960s of institutional support for key partners. In the 2010s, however, these partners were now NGOs rather than government or universities.

The other key element of the Walker period, which is less clearly articulated, is a shift away from international programmes to looking at inequity and inequality in the US. The proportion going to international programmes fell from 40 per cent in the 1990s to between 20 per cent and 25 per cent under Lius and Walker. In response to COVID-19 the Foundation has issued $1 billion of taxable social bonds to enable it to increase its grant making to 10 per cent of its endowment for 2020–2021 (Ford Foundation 2020). The grantees had shifted from government and educational institutions to a more NGO focus. In this regard the Ford Foundation is beginning to look like many other international NGOs.

Conclusion

The Ford Foundation has been distinctive in comparison with both Rockefeller and Gates, the other focus agencies of this book: it has been more flexible to context, and has adapted to change, with a central focus throughout being on forms of less radical social change. In the earlier years this was part of the Cold War agenda and worked closely with partner governments as well as US and local research institutes. That was very much part of the liberal narrative of development at the time. It was also part of the shaping the US view of the Global South through its funding of area studies and development studies programmes at US universities and think tanks.

The work in India exemplified the Cold War approach of strengthening government that may be politically important to the US, but more significantly to strengthen them to take on more liberal views in their own society. It also made major steps in broadening the US elite and policy makers' international world view. It was a very liberal view, and the Foundation sought to steer international debates that broadened US interests, if not the direct interest of the government of the day.

Notes

1 The phrase 'A year of Social Change' has been on the front of the online versions of the Annual Report from 1950 until 2005 to encapsulate this shift in values. Since 2005 the message is essentially the same but the phrasing changes, possibly to make it more contemporary, and less of a slogan.
2 These dividends paid were the highest paid to the Foundation at the time: $15.4 million in 1948, $13.9 million in 1949, $68 million in 1950, and $51 million in 1951 (~$500 million in 2019 dollars) (Sutton 1987, p. 52).
3 https://www.fordfoundation.org/work/our-grants/grants-database/grants-all

4 For UNESCO it was Ukraine refugees in 1951 and UNHCR for Hungarian refuges in 1957.
5 Johnson had a difficult relationship with Prime Minister Indira Gandhi, culminating with him withholding food aid over her views on the war in Vietnam (Kilby 2017, 2019).

References

Arnove, Robert, and Nadine Pined. 2007. 'Revisiting the "big three" foundations.' *Critical Sociology* 33 (33).

Aurora, Bhavan Vij. 2015. 'Ford Foundation Put under MHA Watch List in "National Interest and Security" of India'. *Economic Times*, April 25.

Banerji, D. 1976. 'Will Forcible Sterilisation Be Effective?' *Economic and Political Weekly* 11 (18): 665–665.

Bang, Thakurdas, and Ramabhai Suresh. 1952. 'The Truth About Etawah.' *Economic and Political Weekly* 4 (22): 449–452.

Barker, Michael 2008. 'The Liberal Foundations of Environmentalism: Revisiting the Rockefeller-Ford Connection.' *Capitalism Nature Socialism* 19 (2): 15–42.

Bell, David. 1968a. Memo to George Bundy George March 12. Office of the Vice-President Frances Sutton Series II: Ford Foundation Archives program files Asia-CIA 1952–1982 Box 14, Folder 10. Rockefeller Archive Center, Tarrytown NY.

Bell, David. 1968b. Memo: to George Bundy, Sept 33. Office of the Vice-President Frances Sutton Series II: Ford Foundation Archives program files Asia-CIA 1952–1982 Box 14, Folder 11. Rockefeller Archive Center, Tarrytown NY.

Bell, Peter D. 1971. 'The Ford Foundation as a transnational actor.' *International Organization* 25: 465–478.

Berman, Edward H. 1983. *The influence of the Carnegie, Ford, and Rockefeller Foundations on American foreign policy: The ideology of philanthropy.* Albany, NY: SUNY Press.

Bresnan, John, and Robert Edwards. 1968. Memo to David Bell David Jan 24. Office of the Vice-President Frances Sutton Series II: Ford Foundation Archives program files Asia-CIA 1952–1982 Box 14, Folder 10. Rockefeller Archive Center, Tarrytown NY.

Bridges, Hal. 1958. 'The robber baron concept in American history'. *Business History Review* 32 (1): 1–13.

Bundy, McGeorge. 1972. 'President's Review: Annual Report'. New York: Ford Foundation.

Bundy, McGeorge. 1974. 'President's Review: Annual Report'. New York: Ford Foundation.

Bundy, McGeorge. 1977. 'President's Review: Annual Report'. New York: Ford Foundation.

Bundy, McGeorge. 1978. 'President's Review: Annual Report'. New York: Ford Foundation.

Caldwell, John, and Pat Caldwell. 1986. *Limiting population growth and the Ford Foundation contribution*. London: Frances Pinter.

Czernecki, Igor. 2013. 'An intellectual offensive: The Ford Foundation and the destalinization of the Polish social sciences.' *Cold War History* 13 (3): 289–310.

Dressner, Howard. 1971. Mermo: to Exec Officers, Jan 20. Office of the Vice-President Frances Sutton Series II: Ford Foundation Archives Program Files 1969–1981. Box 23 Folder 5. Rockefeller Archive Center, Tarrytown NY.

Dressner, Howard. 1972. Memo to Bundy and others March 6, Grant Payments. Office of the Vice-President Frances Sutton Series II: Ford Foundation Archives Program Files 1969–1981. Box 23 Folder 3. Rockefeller Archive Center, Tarrytown NY.

Edwards, Michael. 2019. Interview Sept 26.

Ensminger, Douglas. 1955. Letter to Gaither Dec 26. In The Office of President H Rowan Gaither, Area 1. The establishment of Peace Program Material: Ford Foundation Archives, Group 21 Box 1, Series 1, Folder 6. Rockefeller Archive Center, Tarrytown NY.

Ensminger, Douglas. 1956. Letter to Gaither July 3. The Office of President H Rowan Gaither, Area 1. The establishment of Peace Program Material: Ford Foundation Archives, Group 21 Box 1, Series 1, Folder 8. Rockefeller Archive Center, Tarrytown NY.

Finkelstein, David 1969. Memo: to Sutton re China Program, March 28. Office of the Vice-President Frances Sutton Series II, edited: Ford Foundation Archives program files Asia The Pacific: China Box 12, Folder 5. Rockefeller Archive Center, Tarrytown NY.

Ford, Henry II. 1976. Letter of Resignation by Henry Ford II: Upon his departure from the board of trustees of the Ford Foundation. Foundation News/Philanthropy Roundtable.

Ford Foundation. 1950. 'Annual Report'. New York: Ford Foundation.

Ford Foundation. 1957. News from the Ford Foundation April 22 Records office of the President, Office Files of Henry T Heald FA622: Ford Foundation Archives, Group 22 Box 5, Series 1, Folder 65, Subject India General. Rockefeller Archive Center, Tarrytown NY.

Ford Foundation. 1960a. 'Annual Report'. New York: Ford Foundation.

Ford Foundation. 1960b. 'Report: Food Production in India. Records office of the President', Office Files of Henry T Heald FA622: Ford Foundation Archives, Group 22 Box 5, Series 1, Folder 66, Subject India General. Rockefeller Archive Center, Tarrytown NY.

Ford Foundation. 1962. 'Annual Report'. New York: Ford Foundation.

Ford Foundation. 1966. 'Ford Motor Car Co complaints about Ford Foundation activities'. Office of the President George Bundy Series II: Ford Foundation Archives Subject Files Ford-Human Rights Box 15, Series 1, Folder 186 Rockefeller Archive Center, Tarrytown NY.

Ford Foundation. 1967. 'Annual Report, 1966'. New York: Ford Foundation.

Ford Foundation. 1970. Memo, Kennedy to Executive Officer Jan 21. Office of the Vice-President Frances Sutton Series II: Ford Foundation Archives

Program Files 1969–1981. Box 23 Folder 5. Rockefeller Archive Center, Tarrytown NY.

Ford Foundation. 1971. 'The Ford Foundation and the study of China'. Information paper, June. In Office of the Vice-President Frances Sutton Series II: Ford Foundation Archives program files Asia 1967–1981 contd Box 13, Folder 1. Rockefeller Archive Center, Tarrytown NY.

Ford Foundation. 1980. 'Report of Ford Foundation Rural Economy Team visit to China', October. In Office of the Vice-President Frances Sutton Series II: Ford Foundation Archives program files Asia 1967–1981 contd Box 13, Folder 2. Rockefeller Archive Center, Tarrytown NY.

Ford Foundation. 2020. 'Ford Foundation Takes Historic, Unprecedented Action to Increase Grantmaking for Nonprofits by $1 Billion with Proceeds of Offering of Social Bonds in Response to COVID-19'. June 11. https://www.fordfoundation.org/the-latest/news/ford-foundation-takes-historic-unprecedented-action-to-increase-grantmaking-for-nonprofits-by-1-billion-with-proceeds-of-offering-of-social-bonds-in-response-to-covid-19/.

Fosdick, Raymond B. 1952. *The Story of the Rockefeller Foundation*. New York: Harper and Brothers.

Hauptmann, Emily. 2012. 'The Ford Foundation and the rise of behavioralism in political science'. *Journal of the History of the Behavioral Sciences* 48 (2): 154–173.

Heald, Henry. 1963. Memo: Heald to 'Frosty' F Hill May 3. In Records Office of the President, Office Files of Henry T Heald International Affairs: Ford Foundation Archives, Group 22 Box 6, Series 1, Folder 72, Subject India General. Rockefeller Archive Center, Tarrytown NY.

Hertz, Willard. 1970a. Memo to William R Cotter, Sept 18, Grant payment in Ford Stock. In Office of the Vice-President Frances Sutton Series II: Ford Foundation Archives Program Files 1969–1981. Box 23 Folder 5. Rockefeller Archive Center, Tarrytown NY.

Hertz, Willard. 1970b. Memo to William R Cotter, Sept 25, Grant payment in Ford Stock. In Office of the Vice-President Frances Sutton Series II: Ford Foundation Archives Program Files 1969–1981. Box 23 Folder 5. Rockefeller Archive Center, Tarrytown NY.

Huo, Shuhong, and Inderjeet Parmar. 2019. 'A new type of great power relationship? Gramsci, Kautsky and the role of the Ford Foundation's transformational elite knowledge networks in China'. *Review of International Political Economy* 27 (2): 234–257.

Hutchins, Robert. 1953. Memo: Hutchins to Gaither April 13, Draft for a presentation to the Trustees on Area 1. The Office of President H Rowan Gaither, Area 1. The establishment of Peace Program MaterialI: The Ford Foundation Archives Group 21 Box 1 series 1 Folder 5: Rockefeller Archive Center, Tarrytown NY.

Isaacs, Norman 1958. Letter to Mark Etheridge, June 2. Records office of the President, Office Files of Henry T Heald FA622: Ford Foundation Archives, Group 22 Box 5, Series 1, Folder 65, Subject India General. Rockefeller Archive Center, Tarrytown NY.

Kilby, Patrick. 2006. 'Accountability for Empowerment: Dilemmas Facing Non-Governmental Organizations'. *World Development* 34 (6): 951–63.

Kilby, Patrick. 2017. 'China and the United States as Aid Donors: Past and Future Trajectories'. *Policy Studies* 77. Honolulu: East West Center.

Kilby, Patrick. 2019. *The Green Revolution: narratives of politics, technology and gender.* Abingdon: Routledge.

Laski, Harold. 1930. 'Foundations, universities and research'. In Harold Laski, *The dangers of obedience and other essays,* 153–171. New York: Harper and Brothers.

Lele, Uma, and Arthur A.Goldsmith. 1989. 'The Development of National Agricultural Research Capacity: India's Experience with the Rockefeller Foundation and Its Significance for Africa.' *Economic Development and Cultural Change* 37 (2): 305–343.

Lerner, Adam B. 2018. 'Political Neo-Malthusianism and the Progression of India's Green Revolution.' *Journal of Contemporary Asia*: 1–23.

Lin, Justin Yifu. 2011. 'New structural economics: A framework for rethinking development.' *The World Bank Research Observer* 26 (2):193–221.

Loveridge, Jack. 2017. 'Between hunger and growth: pursuing rural development in Partition's aftermath, 1947–1957.' *Contemporary South Asia* 25 (1): 56–69.

Macdonald, Dwight. 1955(2017). *Ford Foundation: The Men and the Millions.* London: Routledge.

Magat, Richard. 1978. Memo to Bell, Dressner and Sutton re Franklin Publication, Dec 15. In Office of the Vice-President Frances Sutton Series II: Ford Foundation Archives program files Asia-CIA 1952–1982 Box 14, Folder 10. Rockefeller Archive Center, Tarrytown NY

Magat, Richard. 1979. *The Ford Foundation at Work: Philanthropic Choices. Methods and Style.* New York and London: Plenum Press.

Mallet, Victor 2015. 'India targets Ford Foundation as national security risk'. *Financial Times.* April 24.

Marquez, Benjamin. 2020. 'Trial by fire: the Ford Foundation and MALDEF in the 1960s'. *Politics, Groups, and Identities.* 8:4, 661-676.

Martin, Ian. 1971. The Ford Foundation in India and Pakistan, 1952–1970, Oct. 8 In Reports 001970: Ford Foundation Digital archive, Rockefeller Archive Center, Tarrytown NY.

McCarthy, Kathleen. 1984. 'US Foundations and International Concerns'. In *Philanthropy and Culture: the international Foundation Perspective,* edited by Kathleen McCarthy. Philadelphia: University of Pennsylvania Press.

McGhee, George 1951. Letter to Hoffman Feb 9, (as ass sec of state) seeking support for Near East Foundation In The Office of President H Rowan Gaither, Area 1. The establishment of Peace Program Material: Ford Foundation Archives, Group 21 Series 1, Folder 4. Rockefeller Archive Center, Tarrytown NY.

Micinski, Nicholas R. 2017. 'The Changing Role of the Ford Foundation in International Development, 1951–2001'. *Voluntas* 28 (3): 1301–1325.

MItra, Devirupa, and Anuj Srivas. 2016. 'Revealed: How Ford Foundation Got the Modi Government to Back Off From Its Expulsion Move, October 26'. *The Wire.* https://thewire.in/diplomacy/revealed-how-ford-foundation-got-the-modi-government.

Nemchenok, Victor V. 2009. '"That So Fair a Thing Should Be So Frail:" The Ford Foundation and the Failure of Rural Development in Iran, 1953–1964'. *Voluntas* 63 (2): 261–284.

Nielsen, Waldemar A. 1972. *The Big Foundations.* New York: Columbia University Press.

Passin, Herbert 1968. Memo to David Finkelstein Feb 20. In Office of the Vice-President Frances Sutton Series II: Ford Foundation Archives program files Asia The Pacific: China Box 12, Folder 5. Rockefeller Archive Center, Tarrytown NY.

Pennington, Hilary. 2020. 'A Message of Support for Our Grantees'. Equals Change Blog. 2020. https://www.fordfoundation.org/ideas/equals-change-blog/posts/a-message-of-support-for-our-grantees/.

Perkins, John H. 1990. 'The Rockefeller Foundation and the green revolution, 1941–1956'. *Agriculture and Human Values* 7 (3–4):6–18.

Robinson, Marshall. 1979. Memo to George Bundy, George May 23, 'China and the Ford Foundation an open door'. In Office of the Vice-President Frances Sutton Series II: Ford Foundation Archives program files Asia The Pacific: China Box 12, Folder 6. Rockefeller Archive Center, Tarrytown NY.

Roelofs, Joan. 2003. *Foundations and public policy: The mask of pluralism.* Albany, NY: SUNY Press.

Roelofs, Joan. 2007. 'Foundations and collaboration.' *Critical Sociology* 33 (3): 479–504.

Rosenfield, Patricia, and Rachel Wimpee. 2015. 'The Ford Foundation Constant Themes, Historical Variations: 1936–2001'. Rockefeller Archive Center, Tarrytown NY.

Sackley, Nicole. 2012. 'Foundation in the Field: The Ford Foundation New Delhi Office and the Construction of Development Knowledge, 1951–1970'. In *University of Richmond UR Scholarship Repository-History.* Richmond, VA: University of Richmond.

Scott-Smith, Giles 2014. 'Maintaining Transatlantic Community: US Public Diplomacy, the Ford Foundation and the Successor Generation Concept in US Foreign Affairs, 1960s–1980s'. *Global Society* 28 (1): 90–103.

Sorensen, Charles E. with Williamson, Samuel T. 1956. *My Forty Years with Ford.* New York: Norton.

Staples, Eugene. 1969. Memo to Sutton. China Program, June 29. In Office of the Vice-President Frances Sutton Series II: Ford Foundation Archives program files Asia The Pacific: China Box 12, Folder 5. Rockefeller Archive Center, Tarrytown NY.

Sutton, Frances. 1987a. 'Introduction'. In *Ford Foundation: The Men and the Millions*, edited by Dwight. Macdonald. London: Routledge.

Sutton, Francis X 1987b. 'The Ford Foundation: the early years'. *Daedalus* 116 (1): 41–91.

Wilson, Kalpana. 2018. 'For Reproductive Justice in an Era of Gates and Modi: The Violence of India's Population Policies'. *Feminist Review* 119 (1): 89–105.

Wood, Robert Everett. 1986. *From Marshall Plan to debt crisis: Foreign aid and development choices in the world economy.* Vol. 355. Berkeley and Los Angeles: University of California Press.

4   The Gates' Foundation

Introduction

The Bill and Melinda Gates' Foundation, with an endowment of $50 billion and an annual income for disbursement of $3–5 billion is among the largest non-government donors in international development and foreign aid, and accounts for around half of all Western Foundation funding for international development (Fejerskov 2018, p.4).[1] The earlier foundations, Rockefeller and Ford covered in this book, are now shadows of their former glory, due in part to the economic downturn of the 1970s and 1980s that reduced their endowment base, together with their increased focus on domestic US issues.

This chapter will argue that, like the Rockefeller and Ford Foundations of the last century, the Gates' Foundation is not only interested in funding development projects, but also in fashioning and shaping international development policy, particular in the field of health, and to a lesser extent in agriculture. Gates' has done this by funding key initiatives in vaccine research, development, and distribution as well as supporting the universities and think tanks undertaking this research.[2]

While the Rockefeller and Ford Foundations were flag-bearers for capitalism, they worked closely with, and shaped, government policy both in the US and elsewhere. The Gates' Foundation, on the other hand, is more married to private sector approaches, being generally sceptical of governments and their role. Gates' input into to government policy is very much to promote the private sector in the delivery of health services. The Gates' Foundation unlike the other major Foundations is run by the founder and funders. The Trustees are the two Gates family members, Bill and Melinda; the Executive Director of the Foundation; and Warren Buffet, who with Bill Gates and the Microsoft Corporation, are the major sources of funds for the Foundation. This very hands-on approach by the donor Trustees give the

Gates' Foundation a particular 'private sector' view into what it believes are appropriate national policies to promote in education in the US, and health and agriculture abroad. In the very early years the Gates' Foundation preferred to go-it-alone, and did not engage with government policy to any great extent. With the arrival of Warren Buffet of Berkshire Hathaway in 2005, and his billions going into the Foundation, this stance shifted so that Gates' moved to consciously have a voice in national and international policy agendas, and by the sheer weight of funding became very influential (Cohen 2002).

This chapter will focus on the Gates' Foundation's international programme, while recognising it has a substantial programme in the US in the education sector. The focus will be mainly on health but will also look at agriculture and the Gates' Foundation's support of the media, a central part of getting positive messages out and limiting criticisms.

The origins

The Gates' Foundation had its origins when Bill Gates decided to set up two modest Foundations in 1994. Some say it was in response to the bad press about Bill Gates' miserliness, or perhaps it was related to his marriage to Melinda a few months before, and her passion for philanthropic causes such as children's education and health. Bill's mother Mary, a well-known civic leader, was also part of '... directing the attention of [Bill] Gates away from Microsoft and towards the world' (Fejerskov 2018, p.66). The first was the William Gates Foundation, named after Bill Gates' father, with an endowment of $106 million. It focussed on the Pacific Northwest of the US, particularly around Seattle, and aimed to give something back to the surrounding communities that host Microsoft. The second was the Gates' Library Foundation, which aimed at putting computers into public libraries. Later it changed its name to the Gates' Learning Foundation that extended the programme to libraries across the US (Fejerskov 2015, Bill and Melinda Gates Foundation 1998, 1999a). Gates' provided a $200 million cash contribution, which was matched by Microsoft with a $200 million software contribution, so all US public libraries could provide free internet access for their users (Fejerskov 2018, p.66).

This set Gates' apart for the other foundations in that it tied the philanthropic work directly to Bill Gates' corporate work with Microsoft. It may have gone close to the conflict-of-interest boundary between Foundations and their corporate donors, but as no one objected, it was largely unquestioned, unlike Microsoft itself and the antitrust charges it faced (Haffner 1999; Tripathi 2006; Martinson

2001). In an earlier time the scrutiny of the Foundation's links to the founders' corporate links would have been much more intense as the Rockefeller Foundation found out in the 1910s, and the Ford Foundation in the 1950s and 1960s.

The William Gates Foundation was run by Bill Gates Snr, first out of the basement of his home and later out of a small office over a pizza shop in Seattle (Cohen 2002). Gates senior would screen the requests and pass the most interesting ones to his son for his views and decision. One of these responses to Gates senior is said to have included a note from Bill and Melinda about the stomach bug Rotavirus, asking if they could do something about it. They had read an article about it killing hundreds of thousands of children every year from diarrhoea (Fejerskov 2018, p.65). While arguably the most obvious solution was greater investment in public health, the Gates' chose the vaccine development path, and thus set the pattern for the future work of the Foundation.

While the initial work of the two Foundations was to support local education and community assets mainly in Washington State, the rotavirus story led to the grants being broadened to supporting research into global health and population (Bill and Melinda Gates Foundation 1998). In 1999 the two Foundations were merged and renamed the Bill and Melinda Gates Foundation, with an initial endowment of $15 billion (Bill and Melinda Gates Foundation 1999b, p.1). This brought the total endowment to more than $17 billion (Bill and Melinda Gates Foundation 1999a; Okie 2006, p.1085). By 2002 the programme's focus had broadened to 'global health; education in the United States; public access to digital information; and the lives of vulnerable families in the Pacific Northwest' (Bill and Melinda Gates Foundation 2002).

In those early years the need for a broader range of vaccines for childhood diseases not already covered, was identified as a gap that the Gates' Foundation could help fill. This work grew very quickly and expanded into research going beyond the traditional childhood diseases. They were soon funding research into new vaccines to prevent malaria, tuberculosis, and HIV/AIDS. This included a $100 million 15-year commitment to the International AIDS Vaccine Initiative (Bill and Melinda Gates Foundation 2001). In those early years, the Foundation also funded projects to:

- address women's reproductive health needs;
- close the digital divide through the $250 million library programme connecting libraries to the internet and providing them

with digital resources under the slogan *if you could reach your public library you would reach the Internet* (Bill and Melinda Gates Foundation 2002, p 2.);

- open the door to higher education, with a 20-year commitment to support 20,000 students from ethnic and racial communities currently underrepresented in higher education in the US;
- integrate technology in schools through a Teacher Leadership Programme, and a Smart Tools Academy.

The latter three programmes remained mainly domestic with the international focus concentrating on the health and the vaccine programme, which was by far the largest recipient with one third of all grants. This early period was also characterised by a number of initiatives including grants to agencies such as CARE and Save the Children Fund (SCF) for earthquake relief in India and El Salvador, as well as support for a number of HIV initiatives through 2002. CARE, Save the Children, and others were also funded for their ongoing international development programme, as well as some their advocacy work. One of the early NGOs grants was $50m to Save the Children Fund in 2000, for a five-year programme to:

> reduce neonatal deaths in developing countries by focusing on increasing global and national attention, strengthening policies and programs, and improving technologies and approaches available to address this critical need.
>
> (Bill and Melinda Gates Foundation 2000a)

and in 2005 a further $75m over nine years 'to test and evaluate a critical set of newborn health care tools and technologies' (Bill and Melinda Gates Foundation 2005b). By 2003 the funding of the global health programme had risen substantially with large grants going to vaccine research (Bill and Melinda Gates Foundation 2002, 2003b). One example was a three year $10 million grant in 2003 to UNICEF for the development of a Maternal and Neonatal Tetanus vaccine (Bill and Melinda Gates Foundation 2003a).

Advocacy was a central part of the Gates' programme, and even in the early years when they kept themselves fairly isolated from official policy and programmes, Gates' started to support some policy related work by supporting the NGO, CARE USA. This started in 2004 with a series of grants to CARE that over the following decade totalled around $30 million.[3] This support for CARE's advocacy and policy work in international development would continue well into the 2020s

(Bill and Melinda Gates Foundation 2019a). The advocacy work was steadily broadened from just supporting CARE's work, and in 2012 it became a programme area of its own, with a much broader remit, provided funding to a range of advocacy programmes to support policy initiatives.

In 2005, the Foundation launched its Global Development Program, with one of the first initiatives being to extend the digital library programme to developing countries outside the US, with Mexico being among the first, and then extend across a number of Latin American countries (Bill and Melinda Gates Foundation 2005a). This soon faded, due mainly to a lack of interest in recipient countries, and possibly because it was tied to Microsoft (Hafner 1999; Stevenson 2008). The focus of the Global Development Program quickly moved to the delivery of vaccines to complement the vaccine development programme, while the Global Health Program was mainly spent on Western based research into vaccines. The Global Development Program used agencies with field based programmes to deliver vaccines to those who needed them the most. This work started in the late 1990s and early 2000s, and by 2005 it was consolidated into a substantial and more coherent programme.

Enter Warren Buffet

In 2006 the Gates' Foundation's endowment more than doubled when Warren Buffet and his Berkshire Hathaway investment vehicle offered 10 million Berkshire Hathaway shares to the value of $31 billion over a three-year period, thus eclipsing the existing Gates' endowment of $25 billion, making Buffet the largest supporter of the Gates' Foundation. This boost in funding would allow grants to double to more than $3 billion per year, which was on the same scale as a mid-level bilateral donor, but with a much narrower focus (Bill and Melinda Gates Foundation 2006). The condition for the Buffet grants to the Foundation was that he would hold onto the shares in his own trust fund and disperse 5 per cent per year, the legislated minimum, to the Gates' Foundation operational programme. The reason for this stipulation was mainly because Buffet believed that he has a better track record in investment strategies than almost anybody else, and as such he could deliver a greater return to the Foundation (Buffet 2006). Buffet also made it clear the gift was not to be in perpetuity but for around 25 years, much in the same thinking as Gates'.

Gates' also toyed with having advisory panels for the three major areas: global health, global development, and the US programme (Bill and Melinda Gates Foundation 2006, p.3). These panels, however, were to be short-lived and did not survive past the three-year trial period with the high level decision-making remaining with the trustees. The structure of the Trustee Board is what is quite different from the Rockefeller and Ford Foundations (except for Ford in the 1930s), both of which have Boards of Trustees made up largely of East Coast liberal elites. These are quite separate from the founding families, who at best had a token representation. The Gates' Foundation on the other hand wanted to keep the decision-making to a small group of family and business colleagues, which had the effect of limiting a broader and diverse source of high-level input into the Foundation.

The Global Development Program expanded beyond health in 2006 with Warren Buffet's additional funding. The proportion of funds spent on the US programme fell and Global Development grew[4] and broadened with a partnership with the Rockefeller Foundation to create the Alliance for the Green Revolution in Africa (AGRA) for technologically-based agricultural research (Kilby 2019). The focus of the Global Development Program, however, was mainly on vaccine delivery.

Over the following years as the annual grants grew and the focus shifted, with Global Policy and Advocacy broadening to become another major focus from 2012 including funding strategic media partnerships. This new approach to media was important to ensure positive stories continued, and the pesky critics would be more limited in how they could get their stories out (see Laski 1930 on how this works). A further change occurred in 2017 when agriculture was taken out of Global Development and folded into a new programme called Global Growth and Opportunity, together with water and sanitation. This enabled a more specialised focus on non-health sectors to develop their own specialist expertise.

The Gates' Foundation has always courted controversy due to the brash nature of Bill Gates himself, and how he set up of the Foundation; the sheer scale of funding in those early years of the 2000s; and its almost obsessive focus on technology. This focus was based on Gates' own belief in technology-based solutions coming from his time at Microsoft where to him technology could solve almost anything. That this was often at the expense of human processes to achieve the same solution, did not come into it. As Birn (2014) notes: 'in the long term the technical bang may turn out to be far smaller than it could have been through combined social, political, and public health measures' (p10). Public health approaches as an alternative were seldom considered, let alone costed.

[Gates'] has far less interest in institutionalization, health care systems and infrastructure, and does not tolerate, as did the RF in the early 20th century, social medicine approaches.

(p.17)

The other main concern continues to be high levels of control by the family together with Warren Buffet over the Foundation, and a perceived bias towards large US corporations as beneficiaries of the Foundation's largesse (Schwab 2020). Pharmaceutical companies are central to Gates' vaccine development work (Harper 2015; McCoy and McGoey 2011), and as we shall see later in the chapter seem to have a perceived, if not real, conflict of interest when they sit on boards such as the Global Vaccine Alliance (GAVI) from which they receive funding.

The next section will focus on the three main international development programmes as of 2019: Global Health, which is research-based, mainly on vaccine development; Global Development, which is mainly about the delivery of health services, including vaccinations, and family planning services; Global Growth and Opportunity, which is mainly about agricultural development, as well as water and sanitation and microfinance; and Global Policy and Advocacy such as touched on above includes support to NGO advocacy as well as the media directly. In addition, is the Global Fund, a special fund under Global Policy and Advocacy to support a global partnership to accelerate in-country activities to address AIDS, tuberculosis, and malaria epidemics. The Gates' Foundation made a 20-year commitment of $750m in 2011 to the Global Fund 'to provide financial support to country-driven prevention, diagnosis, treatment and education programs working to free the world of HIV/AIDS, tuberculosis and malaria' (Bill and Melinda Gates Foundation 2011). The Global Fund is a mechanism to bring developing countries more closely into the other Gates' health initiatives of vaccine development and delivery. While there is a huge array of projects being funded by Gates', it is those focussing on immunisation which draw the most funding, and in the times of the COVID-19 pandemic, even more so.

Global Health and Development

The Global Health and Global Development Programs together anchor the work of the Gates' Foundation with a focus on the research, development and distribution of vaccines (including existing vaccines) in support of disease prevention. One of the first priorities of the Gates' Foundation in 1999 was to extend the availability of existing vaccines to the world's poorest children, through childhood immunisation against diseases such as polio. This has been the focus of the global programme since the outset, while the domestic programme was on education and access to communications technology for all. The focus is now on COVID-19 vaccine development with Gates' playing a relatively smaller part in a much bigger global effort. Gates' role will focus on vaccine delivery to developing countries with other major players such as the WHO and the World Bank, with which Gates' is a major partner in various vaccine initiatives (e.g. Bill and Melinda Gates Foundation 2009, 2015a).

Vaccines define the Gates' Foundation: there is an almost evangelical belief in the role of vaccines to solve a plethora of health problems, even for those that had stumped researchers for the previous 100 years. After 20 years none of those vaccine initiatives against malaria, HIV, or even hookworm, have shown results. In the same way that Bill Gates believed that computer software could solve almost any technical issues, so could a vaccine solve health ones. A sceptic could ask the question: have the basics of our education systems really benefitted from moving from the slate tablet in primary schools of the pre-1960s to learn arithmetic and the alphabet, to the electronic tablets in the modern primary school to perform the same two functions? Is faster access to information necessarily the solution to effective learning?

Likewise, while vaccines are very good at controlling and suppressing many diseases, eradicating them or having universal coverage is another thing altogether. There is an opportunity cost in not only developing a vaccine, but also in attempting to achieve universal coverage and eradication. The question that remains is whether a well-resourced public health programme can complement vaccinations, or whether universal coverage can make these public health programmes redundant. Evidence, particularly in the era of COVID-19, suggests that there is always a place for public health programmes and campaigns around all diseases, as even those once 'eradicated' often re-appear. This doesn't mean that emerging threats such as SARS or COVID-19 will not benefit from a vaccine, but the evidence is that a well-resourced public health programme is also very necessary to contain these and emerging threats, while vaccines are developed to protect those who can't be readily reached, or have a greater chance of infection.

The first major grant for vaccine development was a $125 million grant in 1998 to the Seattle based NGO, PATH (formerly Program for Appropriate Technology in Health) over ten years to develop childhood vaccines. In 1999 this grew with another $50 million to develop a new vaccine to prevent malaria; $100 million for the vaccination of children, and $25 million to assist with the development of an AIDS vaccine (Bill and Melinda Gates Foundation 1998, 1999). In all PATH was given $1.3 billion in the 20 years since 1998 for vaccine research.[5] In 1999 $25 million was given to Aeras for a TB vaccine, and $18 million to the Sabine Institute for a genetically modified hookworm vaccine (Bill and Melinda Gates Foundation 1999b, 2000b). The hookworm vaccine may have been a nod back to the Rockefeller Foundation's work 80 years earlier, which brought hookworm under control through public health programmes, but hookworm has since returned when these programmes were wound down. (Bill and Melinda Gates Foundation 1999a, 1999b).

This investment grew rapidly so that by 2002 'Nearly half of the global health money has gone to vaccines, including a whopping $750 million to the Vaccine Fund' (Cohen 2002, p.2000). At the same time the Health Division was split into three programmes: reproductive and child health; HIV/AIDS and tuberculosis; and vaccines for infectious diseases, with vaccine development receiving the lion's share. Gates' was also a major donor for the Global Fund to Fight AIDS, Tuberculosis, and Malaria, and continues to be the largest non-government donor by an order of magnitude. The Global Health grants doubled between 2004 and 2005, pushed along by a second $750 million commitment to the Vaccine Fund and support for the Global Alliance for Vaccine and Immunisation (GAVI) (Bill and Melinda Gates Foundation 2005b).

The largest grants were to GAVI with $4.2 billion since inception for the development and delivery of a range of vaccines. In addition to the $1.3 billion to PATH, other large scale NGOs support were to $1.3 billion to Rotary and UNICEF for polio vaccination programmes as well as $1.0 billion to WHO (e.g. Bill and Melinda Gates Foundation 2019b). The WHO funding was important as it gave Gates' a say in global health policy, particularly after the they were formally admitted as a partner to the WHO in 2017, and with that a seat at the table.

> The WHO does not have to truly believe that the Gates' Foundation have no conflicts of interests in global health to accept them as a formal partner. But they need to have a strong motive for including them in such a formalized relationship (in this case it is tempting to conclude this motive is found in the fact that the foundation is amongst the IO's [International Organizations] greatest donors).
>
> (Fejerskov 2018, p.175)

This comes into sharper focus when the US Trump administration formally advised WHO of the US withdrawal from the organisation from 2021. While the change of US administration in 2021 reversed this, the nature of the relationship is by no means certain. Like the Rockefeller Foundation with the LNHO 100 years ago, a US Foundation may be the strongest US voice in WHO's policy making into the future. But it was GAVI which has been the most important investment in global health, and most exemplified the Gates' Foundation 'way'.

Global Alliance for Vaccination and Immunisation (GAVI)

GAVI was established in 2000 as a successor to the Children's Vaccination initiative of WHO and UNICEF, after its funding began to decline in the 1990s, leaving children in developing countries invariably under-vaccinated compared to their counterparts in developed countries. This decline led to a number of meetings initiated by the World Bank in 1998, and a challenge from Bill Gates, that resulted in the existing initiatives being folded into what would be known as GAVI. In January 2000 GAVI was formally launched at the World Economic Forum at Davos with funding from Gates' in the form of a small grant via UNICEF to support the secretariat and manage the fund (Bill and Melinda Gates' Foundation 2000c), followed by a series of commitments totalling $1.6 billion by 2005, to be around half of the total GAVI funding at that time (GAVI 2005). GAVI used the Gates' grants to leverage funds from a range of government and other supporters including a high level of industry involvement (Bill and Melinda Gates Foundation 2005a, p.15).

In 2016 another large five-year grant $1.5 billion was provided to GAVI from Gates' for further vaccine development and delivery, probably to cover delays in 'graduation' of many countries from the existing five-year support arrangement (Bill and Melinda Gates Foundation 2016). Overall Gates' has provided GAVI $4 billion in funding. The Gates' commitments have had a central role in matching grants from other donor, hosting funding conferences and leading specific campaigns such as the pneumonia vaccine funding mechanism.[6] GAVI's role was to introduce new vaccines at affordable prices to cover a range of diseases with an active immunisation program:

> GAVI provides eligible countries with new vaccines, safe injection equipment, and modest financial support, which can be used at the countries' discretion to strengthen immunisation systems. GAVI's commitment is for an initial 5 year funding period.
> (Ruairí Brugha, Starling, and Wait 2002, p.435)

By 2008 the number of vaccine manufacturers from which GAVI was sourcing had risen from one to seven over the five years, and the prices had fallen by around one third, but certainly not enough for a sustainable supply paid for by developing countries themselves (GAVI Alliance 2009). In 2012 GAVI introduced a number of new vaccines which, from GAVI's own reports, stretched health systems, and the reach of the new vaccines was slowing (GAVI Alliance 2012, 2016, 2018). By 2018 there had been no increase in the number of children being reached for their first dose of essential childhood vaccines:

> ... estimates suggest that the percentage of zero-dose children has not gone down since 2010. The bulk of our progress on coverage has come from reducing drop-out rates rather than reaching those who were previously unimmunised.
>
> (GAVI Alliance 2018, p.11)

Similarly, the rotavirus disease burden had not changed since 2015 (ibid). So while many of the results are impressive there have been a number of issues that continue to plague the programme that the lack of increased reach in vaccinations is a symptom of: the lack of support mechanisms for providing immunisation within local health departments; the sustainability of the programme on graduation from GAVI; the displacement of existing vaccination programmes by new ones; and finally, the relative merits of particular vaccines *vis-à-vis* other public health approaches. It is the last concern that is probably the most critical in the longer term. Public health is about ameliorating the effects of diseases and limiting their spread. Despite the suggestions from Gates' and other there is not a trade-off between vaccination and public health, the evidence suggests otherwise. They are complementary strategies, and should be treated and funded as such, rather than been seen as alternatives.

Health systems support

This has been an ongoing source of tension within GAVI. It has been referred to as the Atlantic divide:

> ... [an] enduring tension in the history of international health between vertical programmes, which are often single disease-focused, and horizontal approaches such as primary health care ... [and] publicly funded health systems as part of overall social and economic development that was a cornerstone of the primary

health care ideology enshrined in the Alma-Ata Declaration of 1978.

(Storeng 2014, p.866)

Storeng goes on to quote a health systems expert (p.868) who refers to the Atlantic Ocean separating mindsets on Health Systems Support (HSS) with the Europeans, including the head of GAVI from 2004 to 2010, Julian Lob-Levyt, who argued for more funding for national health systems to underpin and ensure the sustainability of the vaccination programmes. On the other side of the Atlantic was USAID and a vociferous Bill Gates who argued vehemently against such an approach, with Gates saying he '... did not want one cent of his money going to health systems' (p. 868) and his maxim that 'health systems don't kill people – diseases do' (p.869). He staunchly believed that there is a technical solution to almost any problem. HSS had at its peak when around one quarter of the GAVI funding going into it, but in a very narrow way, mainly for the delivery of vaccines, rather than the prevention of the disease through public health (Ruairí Brugha, Starling, and Wait 2002). In 2012 GAVI explicitly required 'countries to link HSS outcomes to immunisation results' (Cambridge Economic Policy Associates Ltd 2016, p.6). As Storeng notes HSS had been reduced to 'a vertical programme within a vertical initiative' (2014, p.870).

In the end Lob-Levyt left GAVI, rumoured to have been forced out, and his health systems support team more or less disbanded. The funding of HSS in the programme was necessary for a sceptical Gates' as both the UK and Nordic countries were major funders of GAVI and supporters of HSS, so funding was retained, but at the cost of being directly tied to vaccination programs.

Programme sustainability

The ongoing sustainability of a programme that introduces new technology is a major issue in almost any field of development, and vaccination programmes are no exception. The GAVI scheme operates by not only supporting developing country governments with introducing new vaccines, but also negotiating very low prices compared to what developed countries are able to do on their own; and then overseeing the delivery of the vaccines, usually by UNICEF. This GAVI-led mechanism is at the heart of the issue of sustainability: the ability of local health systems not only to take over the provision of vaccination services without GAVI and other support, but also be able to use single buyer advantages to access vaccines at an affordable price. In practice, pharmaceutical companies oppose 'single buyer' schemes found in many OECD countries such as Australia, the UK, and elsewhere, as they can force prices down and cut corporate margins. Therefore, it is not only the cost of the vaccines themselves that is at issue, but also the bargaining capacity of smaller nations' health systems after graduation from GAVI.

By way of example, in relation to the vaccines for HiB influenza, part of a common five-in-one pentavalent vaccine, even with GAVI prices for five years after graduation, the cost will still adversely impact a local health programme's effectiveness and sustainability, which is reflected in increased morality rates (Le, Nghiem, and Swint 2016). In Ghana, as early as 2002, it was noted that 'the cost of the new pentavalent vaccine would treble the annual cost of its Expanded Program of Immunisation (EPI) from US$3.7 million to almost $11 million annually' (Ruairí Brugha, Starling, and Wait 2002, p.437). The role of the large vaccine manufacturers versus the smaller ones in developing countries soon comes into play. The large companies have an advantage as they are represented on the GAVI Board, despite the seemingly obvious conflict of interest as the GAVI Board and management may favour Board member companies' own products. These companies also use their position on the GAVI Board to prevent the prices paid by GAVI being published, as it would be a great help for UNICEF and national governments to negotiate their own prices based on GAVI's. An example is the price of pneumococcal AMC vaccine, which has a not publicly available locked in price with large manufacturers (Berman and Malpani 2011).

> GAVI model assumes that ... markets can be 'shaped' not only through GAVI's global purchasing power and the impact of new entrants to the market (notably emerging market manufacturers able to compete at a global scale on quality and price).
>
> (Lob-Levyt 2011, p.2745)

This argument seems to fly in the face of logic, and so it is no surprise that prices are not falling as fast and as sustainably as they expected, putting GAVI under financial pressure (Light 2011). In the case of pneumonia, the cost was $1.7 million per 100,000 vaccinated with 360 deaths prevented, thus reducing the existing mortality rate by 0.36 per cent (p.140). Public health programmes looking at preventing these types of pneumonia were not considered. Light goes on to note that for polio, yellow fever, and hepatitis, more people could be reached, and the diseases prevented at a lower cost, with village level public health approaches.

Whether countries will be able to afford pharmaceuticals even at GAVI prices is in doubt, let alone with the higher prices from individual bargaining agreements.

> The financial resources required from the 14 graduating country governments will therefore need to increase from about US$8 million in 2012 to US$90 million in 2018. These projections assume that countries will obtain GAVI prices after GAVI support ends.
>
> (Saxenian et al. 2014, p.199)

The price of vaccines is the largest of these costs: the GAVI prices of course cannot be assured indefinitely so at some point there will be a blow out in vaccination costs or a reduced coverage of vaccination. There are signs this is already occurring, with stagnant growth in GAVI supported vaccinations since 2015, but more importantly increased costs leading to reduced coverage of those who most need it, the poor and marginalised:

> Rotavirus vaccination is most cost-effective in low-income groups and regions. However in many countries, simply adding new vaccines to existing systems targets investments to higher income children, due to disparities in vaccination coverage.
>
> (Rheingans, Atherly, and Anderson 2012, p.A15)

This means that higher income groups who are less affected by rotavirus are being vaccinated at the expense of lower income groups. The $1.6 billion grant by Gates' to GAVI in 2017 may be related to these trends, with Gates' continuing to support GAVI to keep prices down, but without a clear endpoint, and the real possibility that Gates' COVID-19 responses will leave GAVI short of funding. The other issue is that with this reduced coverage due to cost pressures on the receiving government, there are increasing number of outbreaks of existing childhood diseases such as measles, ostensibly covered by existing vaccination programmes that have been displaced. This is leading to a cycle of ongoing disease epidemics (Oroxom and Glassman 2019, p.4).

Displacement of existing vaccination programmes

The GAVI programme is meant to be in addition to existing long-standing vaccination programmes such as measles and polio, among others. Its aim is to expand vaccination coverage to a broader range of diseases such as some diarrhoeal diseases and certain forms of pneumonia. In addition, there is the associated Global Fund, a programme to provide in-country support to address AIDS, tuberculosis, and malaria, which represent an order of magnitude of diseases more difficult to vaccinate against. These new vaccination programmes invariably put pressure on existing health services and vaccination programmes for the scarce resources and staff to implement them. Another issue is the 'vaccination camp' model used to introduce new vaccines, in which people are brought together in single place to receive the new vaccines. This consumes staff time that is very limited and often takes them away from their existing vaccination work, making any centralised record keeping more difficult.

There is already evidence of a drop in the reach of measles and other vaccines as there is pressure to put resources into new vaccination programmes, particularly prior to graduation from GAVI. While public health support is available from GAVI, it is invariably in the form of in-service training focussing on the GAVI programme, rather than pre-service training for new staff, with ongoing support for them in a sustainable way (Ruairí Brugha, Starling, and Wait 2002; Storeng 2014; HLSP 2009). Finally, the issue of donors supporting these vaccination programmes, rather than public health, puts additional pressure on local resources by virtue of the match funding or other support required by these bilateral programmes.

Other public health approaches

Probably the most important question that neither GAVI nor Gates' can answer is whether the immunisation approach is the most cost effective way of addressing public health problems. As McCoy et al note:

> rather than viewing the hundreds of thousands of child deaths from rotavirus infection as a clinical problem that needs a vaccine solution, a better approach might be to view it as a public health problem that needs a social, economic, or political intervention to ensure universal access to clean water and sanitation.
>
> (McCoy et al. 2009, p.1652)

In Mongolia, when confronted with the cost of Hepatitis A vaccine being the largest vaccine cost for government, the government chose to explore other public health options to deal with the disease

(Saxenian et al. 2014). In high mortality countries: '... severe cases of diarrhoea from all causes were reduced [by] 15% with rotavirus vaccination' (Soares-Weiser et al. 2012, p.3). This evidence of relatively low levels of effectiveness raises the question of the cost-benefit of mass immunisation campaigns, when different public health and hygiene programmes may be more cost effective. What seems to be emerging is a 'dependence' relationship between the health systems and the Gates'/ GAVI drug manufacturers' alliance, the upshot of which is the paradox of increased expectations, poorer coverage, and low outcomes.

For example, in India there was a debate about including Hepatitis B vaccines in the regular vaccination programme, over selective versus universal coverage, and the associated costs. Given the outcomes of integrating Hep-B vaccination into existing programmes has been mixed, India prioritised infant mortality reduction to reduce costs, while GAVI wanted universal Hep-B vaccination coverage to increase vaccine uptake. Another example is the unit cost of combination vaccines, such as pentavalent vaccine, is many times greater than if a single vaccine is applied selectively to address specific issues (Kolås 2011).

Emerging health challenges: Corona viruses and global pandemics

In 2020 the world was hit by a global pandemic of a particularly virulent corona virus, COVID-19. This was not the first corona virus to cause an epidemic: there had also been Severe Acute Respiratory Syndrome SARS in the early 2000s; and Middle East Respiratory Syndrome MERS in 2010. Neither turned into a pandemic and were managed and suppressed through quarantine and isolation measures. Both had high mortality rates: in the case of SARS it was 11 per cent and MERS at 35 per cent of confirmed cases. The issue with COVID-19 is that even though mortality is relatively low around 1 per cent of cases, it is far more infectious and spreads more easily between people, and at an earlier stage of infection, thus it quickly became a global pandemic, and puts a massive strain on health services, with hospital services being quickly overrun.

The Gates' Foundation has been supporting a number of initiatives and most recently donated $250 million in early 2020 to address COVID-19, being the first in a programme of funding for COVID-19 (Bill and Melinda Gates Foundation 2020a). The key piece in the COVID-19 puzzle Gates' is involved in is the Coalition for Epidemic Preparedness Innovations (CEPI), established in 2017 after the SARS and MERS epidemics, with Gates' and a number of countries providing seed funding, and regular contributions (Børge et al 2017). Up until 2020 the Gates' Foundation was one of a number of large contributors of $100 million together with Japan, Norway, and Germany with ongoing commitments. CEPI had Ebola, Lassa, and MERS as its focus in 2018/2019 (CEPI 2018, 2019; Bill and Melinda Gates Foundation 2017b). In early 2020 it was working with a number of vaccines development companies and research institutes for a COVID-19 vaccine and put out a call in March 2020 for $2 billion to fund it. By the end of April half the target was reached, enough to fund to the end of June 2020 (CEPI 2020). An emerging issue that CEPI is facing is the equitable distribution of vaccines particularly to developing countries rather than to the 'highest bidder', given the large amount of public funding in the research (Yamey et al 2020; Kang 2020), and the competing bids for the hundreds of millions of doses of the vaccine required. The COVAX facility, launched by WHO with CEPI and GAVI, is designed to equalise the distribution of successful vaccines when they are developed and make 2 billion doses available by the end of 2021 at an affordable price for developing countries (Hassoun 2020). While Gates' is part of COVAX by virtue of their involvement in GAVI and CEPI, and its ongoing commitments are mainly to vaccine testing and treatment (Bill and Melinda Gates Foundation 2020b), Gates' has had relatively little to say about or support for public health response to COVID-19, which is the only viable response until a vaccine is widely available, which may be some years away.

Global Growth and Opportunity

The Global Growth and Opportunity Programme of the Gates' Foundation focussed on non-health related development, mainly related to agriculture and sanitation. The sanitation program looked at improving sanitation mainly through toilet campaigns with what is referred to as Community Led Total Sanitation (CLTS), as well as the development of a vaccine for enteric diseases. Part of this included a programme to improve toilets with a grand challenge to build an improved toilet. With no sense of irony, the winning toilet cost $1,000 plus instillation per household. Given that the total cost to build a house in a poor area after the cost of the land might be less than that, needless to say the uptake was non-existent (Fejerskov 2018, p.131).

In India, Gates' teamed up with the Modi government to end open defecation in rural areas, and as a result Modi won the Gates' award for sanitation. This award was controversial due to both Modi's poor human rights record in India, and its very heavy-handed approach. This was through the Swachh Bharat Abhiyan (Clean India Mission) programme against open defecation by public shaming, among other things, which prompted a backlash from the community (Doshi 2019; Alluri 2019). Not only are these programmes controversial for the approaches they take, but they also tend to overlook or even bypass the existing sanitation work being done by local groups and NGOs, and often worsen the situation.

Studies have shown that the Gates'-supported sanitation programme has limited effectiveness in combating diarrhoeal diseases, and that any positive effects are largely driven by other local factors and interventions (Whittington et al 2020; Venkataramanan et al 2018). As Zuin et al note:

> CLTS [has] spread under the leadership of influential donors, NGOs, and persuasive practitioners ... Robust scientific evidence played little role in the diffusion of CLTS and the rural sanitation sector remains largely driven by weak evidence.
>
> (2019, p.11)

The health benefits according to Gates' own evaluation work are proving elusive (Rijsberman and Zwane 2012, p.8) and, more broadly, beyond CLTS programmes, better water and sanitation may not be the most central issue for controlling diarrhoeal diseases (Engell and Lim 2013; Cumming et al. 2019). This is not to say there are no clear public health benefits, including broader social benefits to women and girls from water and sanitation programmes, but they are not a silver bullet and should be implemented together with a range of other public health strategies (Burt, Nelson, and Ray 2016).

The largest grantee under Global Growth and Opportunity, however, has been in the agriculture sector, the Alliance for the Green Revolution (AGRA), which has received more than $600 million in grants since its formation in 2006. Like the health programme it also leans on technical solutions led by the private sector and with similar mixed, and sometimes controversial, outcomes.

Alliance for the Green Revolution (AGRA)

AGRA was established in 2006 following a call from the Secretary General of the UN calling for a uniquely African Green Revolution, with funding from the Gates' and Rockefeller Foundations. In 2007 the Gates' Foundation gave $200 million over five years, and a further

$15 million in 2008 to set it up, and after that regular grants totalling over $600 million (Bill and Melinda Gates Foundation 2008, 2017). AGRA was a technology-led approach to increasing crop yields across Africa, with a focus on plant breeding, mainly with existing crops, but also by introducing high yielding varieties of rice in some markets. AGRA also has, what the program calls euphemistically, a 'soil health' programme, which has a focus on increased fertiliser use. While there were initial concerns that the programme was a stalking horse for multinational seed companies, annual reports suggest the focus has been on local seed companies with hybrid varieties, and little if any use of GMOs.

After more than ten years of investment in seed development the outcomes have been underwhelming. The massive gains experienced in the Mexico and Indian Green Revolutions did not eventuate. Annual reports list farmers reached with the programme (AGRA 2014, 2018), but if this is put in the context of agricultural output at a national level, the results point to a low level of uptake (Wise 2017). Wise found that growth was mainly due to bringing more land into production rather than increasing yields as such. While cereal production increased by 33 per cent 'productivity increases, however, accounted for barely half of the increased production' (p.1).

> Of the top maize producing countries, only Ethiopia and Malawi raised production primarily through intensification. Nigeria and Kenya, two of the top five maize producers, saw declining yields, while the third, Tanzania, saw annual yield growth of just 1%.
>
> (p.2)

The production models being adopted by AGRA of improved seeds, monocropping, and fertiliser use are generally not sustainable for smallholder and women farmers. This is due to the relatively high costs of inputs that are borne by the farmer, with an associated risk of poor yields. Without input subsidies the programme cannot meet its objectives, but the use of subsidies and higher levels of government involvement are anathema to Gates'.

> The Green Revolution formula of hybrid seeds and inorganic fertilizer may be showing declining productivity as maize monocultures deplete soils whose fertility is not rebuilt with such narrow practices.
>
> (Wise 2017, p. 3)

The clear message is that a wider range of sustainable practices are required, and the use of high input-hungry hybrid seeds requires a radical rethink aimed at the capacity and needs of the smallholder and women farmers (Kilby 2019).

The reason for the 'success' of the Green Revolution in Mexico and India was strong government institutional support, particularly in India, with a large government extension and irrigation investment programmes in the 1950s, which established a strong enabling environment, for high yielding varieties to be successfully grown. The AGRA programme is predicated on the private sector taking the lead in this, which from their point of view simply is not viable in the less densely populated, low rainfall marginal rural areas, with poor existing infrastructure: features that are found in most African target countries.

> Whereas the original Green Revolution arose on the premise of strong state support, the milieu in which the new green revolution for Africa expands is characterized by the spread since the 1980s of neoliberal political agendas and market-based approaches that have put smallholders under severe constraint.
>
> (Bergius and Buseth 2019, p.67)

As with the health sector Gates' belief in the private sector, and what it can do in a variety of contexts, belies the reality of remote communities, where the 1980s structural adjustment programmes decimated rural communities and their support services. The belief that the private sector can replace government services without subsidies and government leadership can only lead to disappointment.

Conclusion

Over the last 20 years since its inception the Gates' Foundation has operated on such a scale in international development that it has been not only able to provide substantial resources to a number of causes most notably in the health and agriculture field, but also to be able to direct the debates and transform institutions such as GAVI and the WHO by the sheer scale of funding available to them. Like Rockefeller and Ford Foundations, Gates' has been driven by a particular world view. Unlike the other major foundations, the Gates' world view is very much that of the founder, his family, and close friend and fellow billionaire Warren Buffet. While the Rockefeller Foundation was similarly influenced by the family and close friend Frederick Gates (no relation), it quickly moved to an independent board of trustees, most likely due to the bad relations the family had with the public at the time. When Henry Ford II took over the Ford Foundation in the mid 1940s, he quickly moved control of the Foundation to an independent (of the Ford family and company) board of trustees.

While these boards were made up of 'East Coast liberal elites' they represented a broader set of views and, most importantly, took the advice of experts. In the case of the Gates' Foundation the very strong views of Bill Gates himself, used to getting his way, and his almost fundamentalist view of technology as being a solution if not a saviour for most, if not all problems, made him and the Gates' Foundation less inclined to take advice. The results of this approach have not been great. After 20 years of research there have not been any vaccine breakthroughs, and the focus away from public health towards vaccination programmes has put local health systems in developing countries under strain. In the AGRA programme in Africa after nearly 15 years there is also little to show, but in this case a lot of local research capacity has been developed. Vaccine delivery programmes have likewise not had success: the aim of enabling local health systems to access new vaccines at an affordable prices has not occurred.

While there is an argument that billionaires can do what they like with their money, they do receive a substantial tax break to do it, and more importantly, it is hard for governments and the elites in government to say no to the largesse, regardless of how misdirected it may be. Similarly, the scale of funding is also enough to stifle public debate on the most appropriate approaches to health care and disease management. The 2020 COVID-19 pandemic is an important case in point. It was only the immediate public health response that was able to keep the virus at manageable levels in some countries such as Australia and Vietnam, and not others, such as the UK and the US. Bill Gates seemed to relent on his views on public health when, in early 2020, he called for increased investment in public health for disease prevention as well as vaccine delivery; as well as funding for research for anti-viral medications and vaccines, but now through public supported programmes, rather than private ones; but the focus is still on large private sector input (Gates 2020). It remains to be seen how long-lasting this 'transformation' will be.

Notes

1 Global South Foundations such as the Tata Trusts in India and Al Waleed Philanthropies in Saudi Arabia, also operate on a similar scale but it is difficult to get comparable figures due the different reporting regimes

2 Some of the larger ones include, a ten-year $280 million progamme on population health to the University of Washington from 2016; a similar sized ten-year grant to Emory University in 2015 on Childhood diseases (Bill and Melinda Gates Foundation 2015, 2016b).

3 The first was $3 million in 2004 to raise awareness of global heath, hunger and poverty. In 2007 this was extended with a $10 million five year program of advocacy for increased official funding for international health and development, and $8 million in 2013.

4 In 2007 the US programme had stabilised to around a quarter of the $2.1 billion of disbursements, and Global Health to just over one half, and Global Development 15 per cent but rapidly growing, doubling from the previous year (Bill and Melinda Gates' Foundation 2007).

5 This a calculation of all grants greater than $5 million from the Gates' Foundation grants database. PATH received $170 million in 2008 for a malaria vaccine development over ten years and a further $185 million in 2009 for the ten-year programme for RTS,S, and malaria vaccine, and in 2014 a further $156 million for malaria vaccine research over six years.

6 This is a mechanism to guarantee fixed prices for that vaccine from the major manufacturers, for an agreed period. What was to happen at the end of that guaranteed period of funding has never been spelt out.

References

Alluri, Aparna. 2019. '"Toilet Trouble" for Narendra Modi and Bill Gates' 23 September'. *BBC News*, https://www.bbc.com/news/world-asia-india-497386 05 (accessed Dec 28, 2000)

AGRA. 2014. 'AGRA in 2014: Positioning For Rapid Progress.' Nairobi: AGRA, https://www.agra.org/resource-library/annual-reports/.

AGRA. 2018. 'AGRA in 2018: Positioning For Rapid Progress.' Nairobi: AGRA, https://www.agra.org/resource-library/annual-reports/.

Brende, Børge, Jeremy Farrar, Diane Gashumba, Carlos Moedas, Trevor Mundel, Yasuhisa Shiozaki, Harsh Vardhan, Johanna Wanka, and John-Arne Røttingen. 2017. 'CEPI—a new global R&D organisation for epidemic preparedness and response'. *The Lancet* 389 (10066): 233–235.

Bergius, Mikael, and Jill Tove Buseth. 2019. 'Towards a Green Modernization Development Discourse: The New Green Revolution in Africa.' *Journal of Political Ecology* 26 (1): 57–83.

Berman, Daniel, and Rohit Malpani. 2011. 'High Time for GAVI to Push for Lower prices.' *Human Vaccines* 7 (3): 290–290.

Bill and Melinda Gates Foundation. 2020b. 'Statement from the Bill & Melinda Gates' Foundation about Today's Coronavirus Global Response Summit'. Press Release May 4.

Bill and Melinda Gates Foundation. 2020a 'Bill & Melinda Gates Foundation Expands Commitment to Global COVID-19 Response, Calls for International Collaboration to Protect People Everywhere from the Virus'. *Press Release* April 15, 2020.

Bill and Melinda Gates Foundation. 2019a. Gates' Foundation Grants Database. Gates Foundation. https://www.Gatesfoundation.org/How-We-Work/Quick-Links/Grants-Database/Grants/2019/10/INV-002464.

Bill and Melinda Gates Foundation. 2019b. Gates Foundation Grants Database. Gates Foundation. https://www.Gatesfoundation.org/how-we-work/quick-links/grants-databaset, 2019/08/INV-003311; 12/INV-001846; INV-001311.

Bill and Melinda Gates Foundation. 2017a. Gates Foundation Grants Database. Gates Foundation. https://www.Gatesfoundation.org/How-We-Work/Quick-Links/Grants-Database/Grants/2017/03/OPP11572882017/11/OPP1180343.

Bill and Melinda Gates Foundation. 2017b. Gates Foundation Grants Database. Gates' Foundation. https://www.Gates'foundation.org/How-We-Work/Quick-Links/Grants-Database/Grants2017/11/OPP1180343.

Bill and Melinda Gates Foundation. 2016a. Gates Foundation Grants Database. Gates' Foundation. https://www.Gates'foundation.org/How-We-Work/Quick-Links/Grants-Database/Grants/2016/01/OPP1131658.

Bill and Melinda Gates Foundation. 2016b. Gates Foundation Grants Database. Gates' Foundation. https://www.Gates'foundation.org/How-We-Work/Quick-Links/2016/11/OPP1152504.

Bill and Melinda Gates Foundation. 2015a. Gates Foundation Grants Database. Gates Foundation. https://www.Gates'foundation.org/How-We-Work/Quick-Links/Grants-Database/Grants/2015/11/OPP1138782.

Bill and Melinda Gates Foundation. 2015b. '*Gates' Foundation Grants Data Base.*' Gates' Foundation https://www.Gates'foundation.org/How-We-Work/Quick-Links/Grants-Database/Grants/2015/06/OPP1126780 /11/OPP1138782

Bill and Melinda Gates Foundation. 2011. Gates' Foundation Grants Database. Gates' Foundation. https://www.Gates'foundation.org/How-We-Work/Quick-Links/Grants-Database/Grants/2011/12/OPP1019422.

Bill and Melinda Gates Foundation. 2009. Gates Foundation Grants Database. Gates Foundation. https://www.Gates'foundation.org/How-We-Work/Quick-Links/Grants-Database/Grants/2009/04/OPP4890.

Bill and Melinda Gates Foundation. 2008. Gates' Foundation Grants Database. Gates' Foundation. https://www.Gates'foundation.org/How-We-Work/Quick-Links/Grants-Database/Grants/2008/11/OPP51697/Grants/2009/04/OPP4890.

Bill and Melinda Gates Foundation. 2007. 'Annual Report.' Seattle.

Bill and Melinda Gates Foundation. 2006. 'Annual Report.' Seattle.

Bill and Melinda Gates Foundation. 2005a. Gates Foundation Grants Database. Gates Foundation. https://www.Gates'foundation.org/How-We-Work/Quick-Links/Grants-Database/Grants/2005/10/OPP652_01.

Bill and Melinda Gates Foundation. 2005b. 'Annual Report.' Seattle.

Bill and Melinda Gates Foundation. 2003a. Gates' Foundation Grants Database. Gates' Foundation. https://www.Gates'foundation.org/How-We-Work/Quick-Links/Grants-Database/Grants/2003/10/OPP28748.

Bill and Melinda Gates Foundation. 2003b. 'Annual Report.' Seattle.

Bill and Melinda Gates Foundation. 2002. 'Annual Report.' Seattle.

Bill and Melinda Gates Foundation. 2001. Gates Foundation Grants Database. Gates' Foundation. https://www.Gatesfoundation.org/How-We-Work/Quick-Links/Grants-Database/Grants/2001/01/OPP4855.

Bill and Melinda Gates Foundation. 2015b. Gates Foundation Grants Database. Gates Foundation. https://www.Gates'foundation.org/How-We-Work/Quick-Links/Grants-Database/Grants/2015/06/OPP1126780 /11/OPP1138782.

Bill and Melinda Gates Foundation. 2000b. Gates Foundation Grants Database. Gates Foundation. https://www.Gates'foundation.org/How-We-Work/Quick-Links/Grants-Database/Grants/2000/04/OPP633.

Bill and Melinda Gates' Foundation. 2000c. 'Annual Report.' Seattle.

Bill and Melinda Gates Foundation. 1999a. Gates Foundation Grants Database. Gates Foundation. https://www.Gates'foundation.org/How-We-Work/Quick-Links/Grants-Database/Grants/1999/08/OPP33.

Bill and Melinda Gates Foundation. 1999b. 'Gates Foundation Confirms Increase in Endowment, Sept 1'. Press Release.

Bill and Melinda Gates Foundation. 1999c. 'Annual Reports for the William H. Gates Foundation and the Gates' Library Foundation'. Seattle.

Bill and Melinda Gates Foundation. 1999d. Gates Foundation Grants Database. Gates Foundation. https://www.Gatesfoundation.org/How-We-Work/Quick-Links/Grants-Database/Grants/1999/04/OPP201.

Bill and Melinda Gates Foundation. 1998a. Gates Foundation Grants Database. Gates Foundation. https://www.Gatesfoundation org/How-We-Work/Quick-Links/Grants-Database/Grants/1998/08/OPP469.

Bill and Melinda Gates Foundation. 1998b. 'Annual Reports for the William H. Gates Foundation and the Gates Library Foundation'. Seattle.

Birn, Anne-Emanuelle. 2014. 'Philanthrocapitalism, Past and Present: The Rockefeller Foundation, the Gates Foundation, and the Setting (s) of the International/Global Health Agenda.' *Hypothesis* 12 (1): e8.

Buffet, Warren. 2006. 'To Bill and Melinda Gates', Letter June 26.

Burt, Zachary, Kara Nelson, and Isha Ray. 2016. 'Towards Gender Equality through Sanitation Access'. Discussion Paper 12. New York: UN Women.

Cambridge Economic Policy Associates Ltd. 2016. 'GAVI, The Vaccine Alliance Meta-Review Of Country Evaluations Of Gavi Health System Strengthening Support.' Cambridge Economic Policy Associates Ltd.

CEPI. 2018. 'Progress Report'. Oslo. Coalition for Epidemic Preparedness Innovations (CEPI).

CEPI. 2019. 'Progress Report'. Oslo: Coalition for Epidemic Preparedness Innovations (CEPI).

CEPI. *2020.* '$2 Billion Required to Develop a Vaccine against the COVID-19 Virus, March 14'. https://cepi.net/news_cepi/2-billion-required-to-develop-a-vaccine-against-the-covid-19-virus-2/.

Cohen, Jon. 2002. 'Gates' Foundation Rearranges Public Health Universe.' *Science* 295 (5562): 2000.

Cumming, Oliver, Benjamin F. Arnold, Radu Ban, Thomas Clasen, Joanna Esteves Mills, Matthew C. Freeman, and Bruce Gordon et al. 2019. 'The

Implications of Three Major New Trials for the Effect of Water, Sanitation and Hygiene on Childhood Diarrhea and Stunting: A Consensus Statement.' *BMC Medicine* 17 (1): 1–9.

Doshi, Vidhi. 2019. 'Bill and Melinda Gates Foundation under Fire over Award for Narendra Modi.' *The Guardian*, 12 September.

Engell, Rebecca E., and Stephen S. Lim. 2013. 'Does Clean Water Matter? An Updated Meta-Analysis of Water Supply and Sanitation Interventions and Diarrhoeal Diseases.' *The Lancet* 381 (17–19 June): S44.

Fejerskov, Adam Moe. 2015. 'From Unconventional to Ordinary? The Bill and Melinda Gates Foundation and the Homogenizing Effects of International Development Cooperation', *Journal of International Development* 27 (7): 1098–1112.

Fejerskov, Adam Moe. 2018. *The Gates Foundation's Rise to Power: Private Authority in Global Politics*. Abingdon: Routledge.

Gates, Bill. 2020. 'Responding to Covid-19 – A Once-in-a-Century Pandemic?' *New England Journal of Medicine*, February 28.

GAVI Alliance. 2005. 'Combined Financial Statements for the Year Ended December 31'. c/o UNICEF Geneva: GAVI.

GAVI Alliance. 2009. 'Progress Report 2009' Geneva: GAVI, https://www.agra.org/resource-library/annual-reports/.

GAVI Alliance. 2012. 'Progress Report'. Geneva: GAVI, https://www.agra.org/resource-library/annual-reports/.

GAVI Alliance. 2016. 'Progress Report'. Geneva: GAVI, https://www.agra.org/resource-library/annual-reports/.

GAVI Alliance. 2018. 'Progress Report'. Geneva: GAVI, https://www.agra.org/resource-library/annual-reports/.

Hafner, Katie. 1999. 'Gates' Library Gifts Arrive, But With Windows Attached'. *New York Times*, February 21.

Harper, Mathew. 2015. 'Bill And Melinda Gates Foundation Makes Its Largest Ever Equity Investment In A Biotech Company'. *Forbes*, March 5.

Hassoun, Nicole. 2020. 'What Is COVAX and Why Does It Matter for Getting Vaccines to Developing Nations? ' *The Conversation*, April 3.

HLSP. 2009. 'GAVI Health Systems Strengthening Support Evaluation Full Evaluation Report'. RFP-0006–0008, Volume 2.

Kang, Ishupal. 2020. 'Who Makes and Who Benefits: CEPI and the Global Effort for COVID19 Vaccine?' *Discover Society – Covid-19 Chronicles*, May 12.

Kilby, Patrick. 2019. *The Green Revolution: Narratives of Politics, Technology and Gender*. Abingdon: Routledge.

Kolås, Å. 2011. 'GAVI and Hepatitis B Immunisation in India.' *Global Public Health* 6 (1): 28–40.

Laski, Harold. 1930. 'Foundations, Universities and Research'. In *The Dangers of Obedience and Other Essays*, 153–171. New York: Harper and Brothers.

Le, Phuc, Van T. Nghiem, and J. Michael Swint. 2016. 'Post-GAVI Sustainability of the Haemophilus Influenzae Type b Vaccine Program: The

Potential Role of Economic Evaluation.' *Human Vaccines & Immunotherapeutics* 12 (9): 2403–2405.

Light, Donald W. 2011. 'Saving the Pneumococcal AMC and GAVI.' *Human Vaccines* 7 (2): 138–141.

Lob-Levyt, Julian. 2011. 'Contribution of the GAVI Alliance to Improving Health and Reducing Poverty.' *Philosophical Transactions of the Royal Society B* 366 (1579): 2743–2747.

Martinson, Jane. 2001. 'The Day the Gods Smiled on Gates – Microsoft Appeal: the software maker is still branded a bully but the remedy of splitting it in two is history'. *The Guardian*, June 29.

McCoy, David, and Linsey McGoey. 2011. 'Global Health and the Gates Foundation – In Perspective'. In *Partnerships and Foundations in Global Health Governance*, edited by Rushton S., and O.D. Williams. London: Palgrave Macmillan.

McCoy, David, Kembhavi, Gayatri, Jinesh Patel, and Akish Luintel. 2009. 'The Bill & Melinda Gates Foundation's Grant-Making Programme for Global Health.' *The Lancet* 373 (9675): 1645–1653.

Okie, Susan. 2006. 'Global Health – the Gates – Buffett Effect.' *New England Journal of Medicine* 355 (11): 1084–1088.

Oroxom, Roxanne, and Amanda Glassman. 2019. 'Vaccine Introduction and Coverage in Gavi-Supported Countries 2015–2018: Implications for Gavi 5.0'. March. CDG Note. Global Center for Development.

Rheingans, Richard, Deborah Atherly, and John Anderson. 2012. 'Distributional Impact of Rotavirus Vaccination in 25 GAVI Countries: Estimating Disparities in Benefits and Cost-Effectiveness.' *Vaccine* 30: A15–23.

Rijsberman, Frank, and Alix Peterson Zwane. 2012. 'Water and Sanitation Challenge Paper'. Copenhagen: Copenhagen Consensus Center.

Ruairí, Brugha, Mary Starling, and Gill Wait. 2002. 'GAVI, the First Steps: Lessons for the Global Fund.' *The Lancet* 359 (9304): 435–438.

Saxenian, Helen, Robert Hecht, Miloud Kaddar, Sarah Schmitt, Theresa Ryckman, and Santiago Cornejo. 2014. 'Overcoming Challenges to Sustainable Immunization Financing: Early Experiences from GAVI Graduating Countries.' *Health Policy and Planning* 30 (2): 197–205.

Soares-Weiser, Karla, Harriet MacLehose, HannaBergman, IritBen-Aharon, SukrtiNagpal, EladGoldberg, FemiPitan, and Nigel Cunliffe. 2012. 'Vaccines for Preventing Rotavirus Diarrhoea: Vaccines in Use'. *Cochrane Database of Systematic Reviews* 11.

Stevenson, Siobhan. 2009. 'Digital Divide: A Discursive Move Away from the Real Inequities'. *The Information Society* 25 (1): 1–22.

Storeng, Katerini T. 2014. 'The GAVI Alliance and the "Gates Approach" to Health System Strengthening'. *Global Public Health* 9 (8): 865–879.

Schwab, Tim. 2020. 'Bill Gates''s Charity Paradox'. *The Nation*, March 17.

Tripathi, Salil. 2006. 'Could the Gates Foundation Do Harm? Salil Tripathi'. *The Guardian*, 5 July.

Venkataramanan, Vidya, Jonny Crocker, Andrew Karon, and Jamie Bartram. 2018. 'Community-Led Total Sanitation: A Mixed-Methods Systematic Review of Evidence and Its Quality'. *Environmental Health Perspectives* 126 (2): 026001(1–14).

Whittington, Dale, Mark Radin, and Marc Jeuland. 2020. 'Evidence-Based Policy Analysis? The Strange Case of the Randomized Controlled Trials of Community-Led Total Sanitation'. *Oxford Review of Economic Policy* 36 (1): 191–221.

Wise, Timothy A. 2017. 'AGRA at Ten Years: Searching for Evidence of a Green Revolution in Africa'. Kampala, Uganda: Alliance for Food Security in Africa.

Yamey, Gavin, Marco Schäferhoff, Richard Hatchett, Muhammad Pate, Feng Zhao, and Kaci Kennedy McDade. 2020. 'Ensuring Global Access to COVID-19 Vaccines'. *The Lancet* 395 (10234): 1405–1406.

Zuin, Valentina, Caroline Delaire, Rachel Peletz, Alicea Cock-Esteb, Ranjiv Khush, and Jeff Albert. 2019. 'Policy Diffusion in the Rural Sanitation Sector: Lessons from Community-Led Total Sanitation (CLTS)'. *World Development* 124 (104643): 1–14.

5 Conclusion

The state of foundations in a COVID world and the rise of the Global South

Introduction

The story of the large philanthropic foundations, Rockefeller, Ford, and Gates', over the past 100 years is a story of idealism, naivety, self-interest, hegemony, and bullying. It is how these elements intersect that makes drawing any definitive judgement on the effectiveness of these foundations in international development so difficult: like the proverbial curate's egg 'they are good in parts'. Many critics of foundations see them collectively as vehicles to advance capitalism and support liberal democracy as an 'ideal' form of societal government (McGoey 2012, 2015; Berman 1983; Barker 2008; Arnove and Pined 2007; Edwards 2009; Morvaridi 2012). A new chapter in this story is the emerging role of the foundations from the Global South, and because of their location probably more than anything else they are quite different to the legacy foundations of Rockefeller, Ford, and Gates'. This chapter will explore their emergence in the context of a possible declining role for the western foundations during the COVID-19 pandemic and its likely aftermath.

One emerging issue for all foundations, Southern foundations as well as those from the West, is the natural tendency of the very wealthy to surround themselves with like-minded thinkers. This leads to a form of group-think, which Spires refers to as 'homophily', gravitating to 'the sorts of outlooks, attitudes, and beliefs that people share in friendships and political affiliations' (Spires 2011, p.308), and in the US Edwards (2019) refers to a dominance of the US East Coast liberal elites having a similar effect. What is notable is that it is only in recent years that boards of trustees of western philanthropic foundations have begun to have southern (albeit elite) voices represented: Ford has trustees from Colombia and Nigeria, and Rockefeller has trustees from Rwanda, China, and also Nigeria. Gates', like many others, is still very much guided by the founders and funders who have the main say, and while not necessarily an East Coast liberal elite they may represent a US West Coast technocratic elite.

For a long time, arguably still the case with Gates', the lack of Southern voices and more to the point for the others, means there is a need to move beyond elites in law, business, and finance, to have a clearer understanding of real local voices. Elite technocratic solutions may not work well in local contexts and their particular social milieu. The COVID-19 crisis and its effect on the Global South will force changes in how existing foundations operate and offer opportunities for the newer emerging foundations. For them to be successful a closer engagement with the local is essential.

The foundations of the Global South

Given the pre-eminence of US foundations for the past 100 years, this story has an American flavour. However, the challenge in the COVID-19 world of the 2020s, dominated by deep recession, a global public health crisis, and an overarching uncertainty of what will come next, the space for US foundations will most likely narrow, and opportunities for those foundations from the Global South will emerge. Managing the COVID outbreak will involve much more than vaccines, including increased support for public health as well as longer term anti-poverty programmes. Rockefeller and Ford are shadows of their former selves, and the resource strain on Gates' and its dedicated focus on medical solutions (Rummier 2020), suggests the future, one way or another, may be from the Global South. The signs are there with the Al Waleed Philanthropies, the Tata Trusts, and the emerging Chinese foundations among many other smaller foundations that can pick up the slack, while at the same time challenging the idea of foundations as being part of a Western liberal conspiracy,[1] but now the liberal elites are local.

Alwaleed Philanthropies

The Alwaleed Philanthropies is typical of the newer emerging foundations from the Global South. They are the second largest philanthropic foundation after the Gates' Foundation: it was formed as three interrelated foundations in 1980 by Al-Waleed bin Talal and Princess Ameerah (Schuyt, Hoolwerf, and Verkaik 2017, p.72), and in 2015 they were merged into one with the promise of all of Bin Talal's $32 billion going into it (Stall 2016). It disburses around $750 million per year to UN agencies and a range of NGOs across 160 countries' NGOs (Dickinson 2017), with its President Bin Talal being the only Arab billionaire to sign up to the Giving Pledge led by Bill Gates and Warren Buffet (El Taraboulsi-McCarthy 2017, p.9). The international focus of Al Waleed is providing philanthropy:

> ... without boundaries' – regardless of race or religion ... across four focus areas: ensuring cultural understanding, developing communities, empowering women and young people, and providing vital relief in times of crisis.
>
> (Alwaleed Philanthropies 2019, p.1)

In terms of the political context surrounding the Philanthropies, Bin Talal himself is a leading figure in Saudi politics, a member of the royal family, and one of the those famously imprisoned in the Ritz Carlton hotel by King Salman in 2017 for not paying sufficient 'taxes' to the King (Al Qurtuby and Aldamer 2018). The Al Waleed Philanthropies lie probably on the more liberal and less dogmatic end of the Saudi political spectrum focusing 'on collaborating, project implementation and grant making, with a strong focus at women and youth' (Schuyt, Hoolwerf, and Verkaik 2017, p.72) and they are increasing their focus on COVID-19 works with an additional $30 million per annum on top of their normal budget (Kane 2020). Al Waleed is less concerned about political ideologies beyond a focus on women's' empowerment, given the fraught politics of the Middle East, but does have a particular focus on Lebanon, where Bin Talal grew up as a boy with his mother and grandmother.

The Tata Trusts

The J. N. Tata Endowment Fund, was established in 1892, and like Andrew Carnegie a few years later, the 'founder' Jamsetji Tata, believed that 'patchwork philanthropy' aimed at welfare to the poor was not a firm basis for his philanthropic work, preferring 'constructive philanthropy' by which 'winners' in the form of the brightest and best young people were picked and provided scholarships for study abroad (Kumar 2018). In 1932 his son Sir Dorabji Tata formed the Tata Trust Fund and he placed all his wealth into it. From this a number of institutions emerged over the following decades,[2] all of which intentionally mirrored in India the 'scientific philanthropy' approach taken by both the Rockefeller and Ford Foundations in the US (Kumar 2018, p.11). The various Tata institutes focus on training and research and less on influencing government policy directly or publicly, but of course they would have had access to officials and ministers and opportunities for influence. The focus is very broad, mainly on national research, such as the India Institute of Science and of Tata Institute of Social Sciences both dating back to the early part of the 20th century. Now there are also programmes in health care, education, livelihoods, nutrition, the arts etc. Like the Ford Foundation in the West the focus has shifted to look at the institutional blockages to access for the poor and disadvantaged to broader opportunities.

What makes the Tata Trust Funds unique is that they hold the majority of voting shares in Tata and Sons, the holding company of the giant Tata group, which is valued at $100b with a staff of nearly 500,000 (Thomsen 2011, p.4). The annual distribution of around $2 billion from a number of funds in both the Sir Ratan Tata Trust, and the Sir Dorabji Tata Trust goes to the full range of activities outlined above. Because of the Trust's majority shareholding in the Tata Group of companies, they can direct a strong focus on corporate social responsibility (CSR) within the group of companies, and usually to the community where the various companies are working, and this is part of the corporate code of conduct (Srivastava et al. 2012). For example Tata Steel at Jamshedpur has a comprehensive programme to support the community as well as the surrounding *adavasi* groups (Shah 2014, p.71). Singh poses the questions as to whether CSR is being responsible to the shareholders (Singh 2008), but of course when the voting shareholders are overwhelming the Tata Trust the answer is moot, as it is being responsive to shareholder needs. This also points out the additional leverage the Trust has with its shareholding and ensuring the philanthropic culture is embedded in the group of companies.

Not only the education programme of the Tata Trusts but also their promotion of CSR through the Trusts' shareholding in the Tata enterprises, challenge the 'hands off' relationships that many foundations have with the companies that spawned them, and might suggest we read too much into our narratives of rampant capitalism being at their heart. There is a tension in achieving the corporate goals of maximising profit while being socially responsible in its work, and the Trusts' goals and having a direct shareholding in the family of companies only goes some way to overcoming that tension.

The emerging Chinese foundations

In China, while foundations are still new and relatively small in scale, the COVID-19 pandemic has enabled the nascent organisations to move more quickly to a global stage. Chinese foundations only became possible to operate on any large scale in 2004 when the law from the 1980s was amended to enable private sector foundations and corporate philanthropy (Shieh 2017; Chan and Lai 2018; Deng 2019). The private Chinese foundations now have similar rules to US foundations, *inter alia* a minimum spend rate of 8 per cent (compared to the 5 per cent in the US), and also tax advantages for the founding company's investments into foundations. Similar to the US, the leadership of these foundations is part of the national elite, and like their US counterparts, broadly support government policy. The heads of the foundations such as Jack Ma of Ali Baba have connections to the Chinese government, and arguably advance the government interests while remaining relatively independent of it at a governance level. More recently these foundations have been moving abroad (Deng 2019), with Ai Baba's commitment to 3 per cent of its turnover to foundation work on top of Jack Ma's '… donation of 23 million Alibaba shares, worth about $4.6 billion' (Doebele 2019 p.1). Ali Baba's founder Jack Ma has also provided over 1 million COVID-19 test kits to most countries in Africa. By April 2020 Chinese foundations had provided $900 million for dealing with COVID-19. This represents around 20 per cent of the global foundation effort at that time (Sellen 2020; Sellen and Joumont 2020).

This growth in Chinese philanthropy is not unexpected with the re-emergence of Confucian philosophy and philanthropic ideals, which has a history dating back a thousand years to the Zhou Dynasty and more recently the Ming and Qing dynasties since the 1500s, where foundations were an important part of the social fabric (Frolovsky 2019). If the current growth rate is an indication and there are tax advantages similar to the US, then it is clear that, as Joumont and Sellen argue: 'China's philanthropic sector will become a force to be reckoned with far beyond its borders in the 21st century' (Jaumont and Sellen 2020, p.2).

Foundations in global development

The role of foundations in global development is contested and largely ignored. They had a role in the early 20th century in keeping the isolationist US committed to the rest of the world through various programmes, particularly in health and international affairs through Rockefeller and Carnegie Foundations' support to the nascent international organisations at the time. In the latter half of the 20th century the Ford Foundation supported the US hegemonic approaches, and ensured its influence went beyond international relations to also have a strong influence on international development and a role in leading US influence on development practice and in-country development directions. The Gates' Foundation, in many ways is a throwback to the Rockefeller work of the 1920s and 1930s, and a technocratic approach to dealing with disease. COVID-19 represents a major change to the development landscape and the role of all donors from both the Global North and the Global South as well as foundations, which can and have played a catalytic role.

In the 2020s while there are a number of challenges facing foundations and global development, two of these come to the fore. The first is an increased nationalism, and this has already impacted the activities of both the Ford Foundation and the Open Society Foundations, and to a lesser extent Gates and some of the vaccine work. The second is more serious, and that is a new wave of poverty and rising inequality sweeping the world, and in particular the developing world. Global and national development over the last 50 years, but the last 20 years in particular, has been driven by increased mobility. While this has been a feature since the industrial revolution in Europe, and earlier in Chinese and other earlier empires, the rate of mobility for work has been staggering. Labour remittances for many developing countries have been a major source of national income. The effect of COVID-19 has been to freeze that mobility in the short term, and certainly limit it in the longer term. Not only will there be public health issues and the inherent risk associated with mobility, but the opportunities will be fewer as the global recession continues to bite and any promised recovery will be slow. This will affect the poor, and poor women in particular. A slowdown in construction will affect men's work while a reduced middle class income will affect women in the service sectors whether it be domestic work or other service industries.

The role of foundations in this landscape will be different: the traditional focus on elite education for marginalised groups, and technical solutions to complex health, social, and economic problems may have less currency in a world emerging from or learning to live with COVID-19. The crisis will be felt for many years if not decades. Foundations typically have not managed these economic, health, and social shocks very well. Apart from the funding of Johns Hopkins School of Public Health, the Rockefeller Foundation annual reports at the time (1917,1918, 1919, 1920) saw the Spanish Flu as causing disruptions to their work, rather than being a challenge to be met. Similar observations can be made about Ford and its participatory development and civil rights work, Soros' work on democracy, Al

Waleed on women's empowerment, and even Gates' and immunisation. They see themselves as having an answer to broader longer-term structural issues to which, in many cases, a technical fix can be applied, and less involved in 'short-term spot fires', even if they appear on a global scale.

In the current pandemic Rockefeller and Ford have focused much more on responses within the US to fill the gap left by government, most certainly at the direction of their boards. Gates has invested it funds on vaccine development, and through GAVI has worked with health care workers, diagnostic tests and surveillance. The Chinese foundations are in their infancy but the Jack Ma and the Ali Baba Foundation have been donating personal protective equipment and hospital equipment across Africa (Sellen 2020; Xinhua 2020). The Chinese foundations will grow quickly and like the US foundations before them, they are likely to reflect broader national strategic interests but at arm's length from government. In terms of programmes, like their western counterparts they are more likely to focus on health and education in a post COVID world, rather than directly funding anti-poverty programmes.

Some final thoughts

What this book has attempted to do is to not only discuss how these foundations have advanced their own interests and world views but also to look at how the Global South has responded to these foundations in a number of different contexts: the Rockefeller Foundation and its work in Asia in the 1930s; the Ford Foundation in India in the 1950s and 1960s; and Gates' more globally in the 2000s. They have all attempted to steer development in certain directions, but what has emerged is a complex picture of attempts at hegemony and domination being resisted and co-opted to varying degrees by their southern partners of independent-minded states and their institutions. Public health in Asia in the 1930s, and the Green Revolution in India in the 1960s are both examples of where the broader intent of the foundation work was subverted to the interests of national government and local communities.

Andrew Carnegie in the late 19th century is credited with being a founder of the ideas and ideals of modern philanthropy (Carnegie 1906), but we cannot ignore the role of Jamsetji Tata also in the 1890s in British India, and his idea of 'constructive philanthropy' (Raianu 2016), both of which were to move away from charity and welfare to provide opportunities for those who don't have these chances. Andrew

Carnegie, with Bill and Melinda Gates 100 years later, was also driven by the idea that the wealthy should give back their wealth, but similar to Tata, not as charity. Carnegie probably reflected on the lucky break in his early teens when he moved from being a bobbin boy in a textile mill to a telegram runner for the railways. This latter role introduced him, via their telegrams, to the rich and powerful and he never looked back. Foundations are guided by the values of their founders, but few of them (Carnegie being the clear exception) have lived experiences to drive their views of philanthropy. It is worth noting, however, that that did not stop Carnegie waging war with his own workers and their unions through the 1890s before he retired in 1900 and became a 'fulltime' philanthropist (McGoey 2012, 2015).

Two major focuses of foundations over the last 100 years have been health and education. In both cases they were very much Western driven and about extending Western ideas of development to developing countries. In health, the Rockefeller Foundation through the League of Nations Health Organisation had a profound impact on the direction of the organisation and moved it down a technology path, with vaccine development and technology getting priority over public health. The exception was in the 1930s when the Foundation's field offices could hold sway and were better able to respond to local needs, such as in Asia, where the field office staff had an important influence on regional governing agenda-making in public health over the following decades (Akami 2017, p.15). Similarly in the 2010s, the Gates Foundations has a seat at the table of LNHO's successor, the WHO, as a major funder is an American voice in WHO deliberations. Like Rockefeller before, Gates' is also very much about private sector led vaccine development and delivery, generally at the expense of public health, which involves in Gates' mind, 'wasteful' governments. The COVID-19 health crisis, which is very much a public health challenge may have some effect on those views, but the ideology of small governments, and technology provided by big business and delivered by the private sector is a very powerful driver for the large US philanthropic Foundations (Edwards 2009).

While the Gates' Foundation is still playing an important role in funding COVID-19 vaccine development, the 2020s COVID-19 recession may impact on the broader resources that Gates and Buffet can provide for the future work of the Foundation. Like the 'stagflation' period of the 1970s on Rockefeller and Ford's resources, and in the 2009 recession for Gates', there is likely to be some impact on the Gates' Foundation's income, which may benefit from a technology boom, but also suffer from declining returns from other investments.

How deep this effect will be it is too early to say, and how much and for how long Gates' and Buffet's personal fortune will go into the Foundation is hard to predict (Metcalf 2020; Raj 2020).

Likewise, in education, there has been a strong western influence. In the very early years with Carnegie funding schools in Africa, this had a racist element and sought to deny black Africans the same opportunities in a liberal education as their white colonial 'masters' (Bell 2009; King 1969). This of course changed after World War II when globall, civil rights movements gained traction and foundations realised that had to engage in this social change to remain relevant and, more importantly, have an influence.[3] The other major role in education was in higher education where foundations have a had a profound impact over the past 100 years. The Rockefeller Foundation started this off by providing scholarships to students from the Global South from the 1920s and at the same time set up its medical school in China, and provided other funding for higher education and research institutes in the US and Europe, and also to their colonies (e.g. see Rockefeller Foundation 1925, 1935). Linked to this was Western scholars being placed in these emergent institutions, which had an influence not only on the curricula but also to move them away from British and other European based teaching ideas, in favour of the US (Srivastava and Oh 2012).

Following World War II, the Cold War enabled the foundations' education programmes to have a stronger ideological focus, advancing liberal democracy, as well as technical advances, particularly in agriculture. The Ford Foundation was the leader in this area with university support programmes, placement of western academics in Southern universities, as well as scholarships from developing countries to Western universities. Central to this work was the view that a liberal capitalist based education was not only in the best interests of the recipient, but the donor as well in advancing its geopolitical interests. The other side of this was to use education funding to steer academic disciplines in certain directions that supported liberal democratic values and capitalism as a 'given', rather than as a contested policy option. This has been only partially successful, and outside the US in particular, there continue to be academic debates around ideology and the directions politics should take.

In the 2010s the rise of nationalism and sharper divides between left and right are more in evidence, and foundations are either leaving this space or are battling to have their voices heard, with their legitimacy more often than not being questioned, as the George Soros and the Open Society Foundation are finding. The Open Society Foundations are currently the most aggressive in promoting liberal democracies and advancing respect for human rights. Increasingly the civic space they have to operate in is being narrowed and as we have seen they are either expelled, not allowed to operate, or they are being kept on a 'short leash' in many countries (Clarke 2019). Even the long-standing Ford Foundation is finding itself under scrutiny in countries such as India where advancing liberal causes, even indirectly, is frowned upon by both government and more ideologically or religious focused local groups (Mitra and Srivas 2016). The hostility that foundations such as Ford, and to a lesser extent Rockefeller, felt in the 1950s from anti-liberal groups in the US is now more a global phenomenon.

In health, the foundations, especially Gates', have to recognise a new reality in a COVID-19 world the effects of which may be with us one way or another for several years if not decades. The challenge facing Gates' and others is that the focus on the private sector and vaccines may only be part of the solution, and it is the Southern foundations that may play a key role in that solution. As experience is telling us, very good public health practices are as important if not more important than vaccines and immunisation programmes. If economies are to function and trade to continue, then a new or a reinvigorated form of internationalism is required, and affordable public health, as well as reliable vaccines and treatments delivered on a scale hitherto not considered. The neoliberal ideology of leaving it to the market and private sector to manage still won't reach those most in need in this new world order. There will be competing forces: one being the new nationalism, for which the closure of borders and resisting of free(er) trade will serve to strengthen, against the competing force of the need for a for an internationalism, which is central to a COVID response. The Southern based foundations are already stepping up with Al Waleed Philanthropies shifting its focus to a COVID response and putting in additional funding, together with Ali Baba and the other Chinese Foundations (Sellen 2020; Kane 2020).

Foundations in the global development space have lived through, and to some extent have driven both technological and policy change in key areas of development over 100 years. We can expect that foundations will continue to play a central and at times controversial role. They will move from being Western based, and subject to regulation, to be more based in the Global South and will probably be less exposed to public scrutiny, some by virtue of where they are located. Like the US they will reflect some of the national ideologies that have enabled them to flourish, and similar to Andrew Carnegie and Jamsetji Tata they will see it as part of their social obligations to return what the state has enabled them to achieve. At the same time that may 'buy' a seat at the table to have a say in state and global policies and direction.

This changing order will certainly lead to arguments of propping up a Chinese hegemony, and creating discomfort in the West, much as their western counterparts have been accused of supporting western hegemony throughout the 20th century. The Chinese foundations in the early 2010s were predominantly locally focussed and still very small focussing mainly on local education support, with only a handful of national level foundations. COVID-19 has provided opportunities for them to expand in the international space much like Rockefeller did a hundred years earlier in combatting yellow fever. With the massive expansion of Chinese investment and development such as the Belt Road Initiative, and the international investment in medical technologies from Chinese foundations, this may see increased Chinese foundation work in Western and Central Asia as well as Africa where China development programmes have had a long history.

One thing is almost certain, and that is that the Chinese and Southern foundations will reflect the broad national interests of their home base, given the support and opportunities on offer from the state, but also to varying degrees reflect the interests of their partners where they work. However, they may be hobbled to some extent by elite views of the world and their own corporate backgrounds and interest. What these examples and this volume have attempted to do is to put the rise of foundations in international development over the last 100 years in context, and highlight the important but also complex role they have played, which defies simple characterisations.

Notes

1 For example Azim Premji's Foundation, India ($21 billion), Carlos Slim Holu, Mexico ($10 billion), Patrice Motsepe, South Africa ($500 million), Peter Kellner, Czech Republic ($13 billion).
2 Tata Institute of Social Sciences, (1936); Tata Memorial Hospital, (1941); Tata Institute of Fundamental Research-Mumbai, (1945); National Centre for the Performing Arts, (1966); The National Institute of Advanced Studies, (1988); and the Indian Institute of Science (1909).
3 Gates has been involved in school education but only in the US where he promotes computer technology in learning, and more recently pushes for more charter schools, where controversially, private operators are fully funded to run schools for public education (Edwards 2009).

References

Akami, Tomoko. 2017. 'Imperial Polities, Intercolonialism, and the Shaping of Global Governing Norms: Public Health Expert Networks in Asia and the League of Nations Health Organization, 1908–37'. *Journal of Global History* 1: 4–25.

Al Qurtuby, Sumanto, and Shafi Aldamer. 2018. 'Saudi-Indonesian Relations: Historical Dynamics and Contemporary Development'. *Asian Perspective* 42 (1): 121–144.

Alwaleed Philanthropies. 2019. https://www.alwaleedphilanthropies.org/.

Arnove, Robert, and Nadine Pined. 2007. 'Revisiting the "Big Three" Foundations.' *Critical Sociology* 33 (33).

Au, Wayne, and Christopher Lubienski. 2016. 'The Role of the Gates Foundation and the Philanthropic Sector in Shaping the Emerging Education Market: Lessons from the US on Privatization of Schools and Education Governance.' In *World Yearbook of Education*, 47–63. London: Routledge.

Barker, Michael. 2008. 'The Liberal Foundations of Environmentalism: Revisiting the Rockefeller-Ford Connection'. *Capitalism Nature Socialism* 19 (2): 15–42.

Bell, Fiona. 2009. 'The Carnegie Corporation Decides on Racially-Segregated Libraries in South Africa in 1928: Negrophilist or Segregationist?' *Library & Information History* 25 (3): 174–189.

Berman, Edward H. 1983. *The Influence of the Carnegie, Ford, and Rockefeller Foundations on American Foreign Policy: The Ideology of Philanthropy.* Albany: SUNY Press.

Carnegie, Andrew. 1906. 'The Gospel of Wealth'. *North American Review* 183 (599): 526.

Clarke, Gerard. 2019. 'The New Global Governors: Globalization, Civil Society, and the Rise of Private Philanthropic Foundations'. *Journal of Civil Society* 15 (3): 197–213.

Deng, Guosheng. 2019. 'Trends in Overseas Philanthropy by Chinese Foundations'. *VOLUNTAS: International Journal of Voluntary and Nonprofit Organizations* 30 (4): 678–691.

Dickinson, Eizabeth. 2017. 'Inside Alwaleed Philanthropies' New Global Strategy'. *Devex*, October 3.

Doebele, Justin. 2019. 'Jack Ma Outlines Bold Vision For His Philanthropy Foundation'. *Forbes Asia*, December 2. https://www.forbes.com/sites/jdoebele/2019/12/02/jack-ma-shares-his-plans-for-education-philanthropy-in-china/#dd0dce95c7fc.

Edwards, Michael. 2009. 'Gates, Google, and the Ending of Global Poverty: Philanthrocapitalism and International Development'. *The Brown Journal of World Affairs* 15 (2): 35–42.

Edwards, Michael. 2019. Interview November 24, Tarrytown NY.

El Taraboulsi-McCarthy, Sherine. 2017. 'A Kingdom of Humanity? Saudi Arabia's Values, Systems and Interests in Humanitarian Action'. September. HPG Working Paper. London: Humanitarian Policy Group, Overseas Development Institute.

Frolovsky, Dimitry. 2019. 'China's Philanthropy Boom: Even While Its Billionaire Class Grows, China Is Also Marking a Drastic Increase in Volumes of Charitable Giving.' *The Diplomat*. January 25.

Jaumont, Fabrice, and Charles Sellen. 2020. 'China: Rise of a New Philanthropic Power'. *The Conversation*, February 7.

Jeffreys, Elaine. 2015. 'Celebrity Philanthropy in Mainland China'. *Asian Studies Review* 39 (4): 571–588.

Kane, Frank. 2020. 'IAbeer Al-Fouti Sees Alwaleed Delivering Global Response to COVID-19 Pandemic'. *Arab News*, July 11. https://www.arabnews.com.

King, Kenneth J. 1969. 'Africa and the Southern States of the USA: Notes on JH Oldham and American Negro Education for Africans'. *The Journal of African History* 10 (4): 659–677.

Kumar, Arun. 2018. 'Pragmatic and Paradoxical Philanthropy: Tatas' Gift Giving and Scientific Development in India'. *Development and Change* 49 (6): 1422–1446.

McGoey, Linsey. 2012. 'Philanthrocapitalism and Its Critics'. *Poetics* 40 (2): 185–199.

McGoey, Linsey. 2015. *No Such Thing as a Free Gift: The Gates Foundation and the Price of Philanthropy*. London: Verso Books.

Metcalf, Tom. 2020. 'Bill Gates Gave $519 Million to Foundation Last Year, May 21, 2020'. *Bloomburg*, May 21. https://www.bloomberg.com/news.

Mitra, Devirupa, and Anuj Srivas. 2016. 'Revealed: How Ford Foundation Got the Modi Government to Back Off From Its Expulsion Move'. *The Wire*, October 26.

Morvaridi, Behrooz. 2012. 'Capitalist Philanthropy and Hegemonic Partnerships'. *Third World Quarterly* 33 (7): 1191–1210

Raianu, Mircea. 2016. 'Tata Philanthropy and the Making of Modern India'. *HistPhil*, February 25. https://histphil.org/2016/02/25/tata-philanthropy-and-the-making-of-modern-india/.

Raj, Shubham. 2020. 'Buffett Biggest Loser among Billionaires in 2020, Sceptics Cast Doubts over His Methods'. *Economic Times*, July 6 edition.

Rockefeller Foundation. 1925. 'Rockefeller Foundation Annual Report 1925'. Rockefeller Archive Center, New York.

Rockefeller Foundation. 1935. 'Rockefeller Foundation Annual Report 1935'. Rockefeller Archive Center, New York.

Rummier, Orion. 2020. 'Gates Foundation Will Focus "Total Attention" on Coronavirus Crisis'. Axios Media. https://www.axios.com.

Schuyt, Theo N.M., Barry L.K.Hoolwerf, and Dave Verkaik. 2017. 'Better Together? A Study on Philanthropy and Official Development Assistance'. 2017–No.57, February. *AFD Research Papers Series*. Paris: Agence Française de Développement.

Sellen, Charles. 2020. 'China's Big Donors Are Pitching in to Deal with the New Coronavirus – and Not Just in Their Own Country'. *The Conversation*, April 3.

Sellen, Charles, and Fabrice Joumont. 2020. 'China Billionaires a Force to Be Reckoned with in Global COVID-19 Fight – and More'. *CNA*, April 7 international edition.

Shah, Shashank. 2014. 'Corporate Social Responsibility: A Way of Life at the Tata Group'. *Journal of Human Values* 20 (1): 59–74.

Shieh, Shawn. 2017. 'Same Bed, Different Dreams? The Divergent Pathways of Foundations and Grassroots NGOs in China.'''. *VOLUNTAS: International Journal of Voluntary and Nonprofit Organizations* 28 (4): 1785–1811.

Singh, J. 2008. 'Tight Rope Walk at Tata Steel: Balancing Profits and CSR [Psi]'. *South Asian Journal of Management* 15 (1): 118.

Spires, Anthony. 2011. *'Organizational Homophily in International Grantmaking: U.S.-Based Foundations and Their Grantees in China.'* Journal of Civil Society 7 (3): 3050–3331.

Srivastava, Prachi, and Su-Ann Oh. 2012. 'Private Foundations, Philanthropy and Partnership in Education and Development: Mapping the Terrain'. *International Journal of Educational Development* 30 (5): 460–471.

Srivastava, Amit Kumar, Gayatri Negi, Vipul Mishra, and Shraddha Pandey. 2012. 'Corporate Social Responsibility: A Case Study of TATA Group'. *IOSR Journal of Business and Management* 3 (5): 17–27.

Stall, Leonard. 2016. 'How to Spend $32bn Doing Good, Aug 15'. Al Waleed Philanthropies (blog). https://www.alwaleedphilanthropies.org.

Thomsen, Steen. 2011. 'Trust Ownership of the Tata Group.' SSRN 1976958. Center for Corporate Governance, Copenhagen Business School.

Xinhua. 2020. 'Spotlight: China-Europe Anti-Pandemic Ties Set Stage for Economic Recovery'. *Xinhua*, September 8.

Index

For Product Safety Concerns and Information please contact our EU
representative GPSR@taylorandfrancis.com
Taylor & Francis Verlag GmbH, Kaufingerstraße 24, 80331 München, Germany